Writer's Guide to Character Emotion

Writer's Guide to Character Emotion

A revolutionary handbook on how to use "Deep POV"

Sherry Soule

FWT

Writer's Guide to Character Emotion
ISBN 978-1502497871

Typesetting services by BOOKOW.COM

For fiction writers who yearn to take their writing skills to the next level!

CONTENTS

INTRODUCTION

Dear Writer,

I thought I'd share a little bit about myself, and why I wanted to create this handbook on self-editing character emotion and expression by use of the Deep POV method.

First off, I love discovering new ways to improve my skills, and I've learned so much over the years by studying the craft. I've had the honor of working with some of the best editors in the business, and I've taken numerous writing classes and read tons of books on the creative writing process.

And as a freelance editor, I wanted to share valuable editing tips that should significantly improve your chances of publication, help you write a novel that you can proudly self-publish, or teach you new ways to revise your short story into riveting prose.

Recently, I updated this handbook and included even more examples and excerpts. If you're a writer like me, then you need to "see" (or in this case *read*) the text as it should be written in Deeper POV. Reading examples always help me, and I hope they help you, too. (All of the examples have been taken from my own writing.)

With each novel I write, I know that I'm getting better at telling a damn good story. This handbook should either remind you of something you need to work on, or teach you a new method for improving your talents.

This is not a "grammar do or don't," because honestly, mine is not the best, so please don't contact the literary police. I am just grateful to share some of my knowledge with you, so you don't make the same mistakes I've made in my own writing journey.

Just remember that you've been blessed with an incredible talent —*the awesome gift of storytelling!* You have the ability to write amazing stories that capture the heart and attention of readers everywhere, so why not become the best writer you can be?

There is a ton of great writing books and helpful editing blogs out there, so I hope my small contribution to the craft inspires you!

Happy writing,

Sherry

***Creativity Coach*, Fiction Editing Services**

DEEP POINT-OF-VIEW

Deep Point-of-View (POV) is one of the best editing techniques that you can use to take your writing to the next level. This chapter will explain how you can revise filter words used in shallower sentences by transforming the narrative in much stronger and vivid ways.

Even if you believe you've already mastered Deep POV, I challenge you to absorb this handbook and go deeper. It doesn't matter if you are traditionally published, an Indie author, a self-published writer, or you enjoy spending your weekends writing fanfiction, these tools and techniques can help anyone improve their storytelling abilities.

Let's start with what many writers call: *Narrative Distance.*

A writer creates narrative distance (taking the reader out of the story or by reminding them that they're reading a book) when writers insert *filter words* into their writing. Deep POV is a much more direct and intimate way to describe a character's emotions, reactions, and actions. It will bring every scene in your novel instantly alive for your reader. And most importantly, it will keep you from using a weaker form of characterization.

Deep POV kicks writing up a notch by tightening, solidifying, and strengthening a manuscript. As a stellar side effect, many of those annoying problems with "show / don't tell" will fade away like a bad memory.

What is Narrative Distance?

This means that the reader has been distanced, or in some cases, jolted out of the story by author intrusion. The more "telling" a writer does, the more distance they put between the reader and the story, and the less involved the reader will feel about what's happening.

SHALLOW: Shawn <u>noticed</u> that the sky <u>looked</u> dark, and he <u>felt</u> a chill.

DEEP POV: Overhead, the sky darkened and Shawn rubbed his arms against the sudden chill.

Do I want this story to be viewed from afar or be deeply experienced?

Personally, I'm a character-driven writer, so I *love* being inside my character's head. I want to experience their journey firsthand.

But writers often create a narrative distance when they consciously or unconsciously insert filter words into the narrative.

This issue is also known as author intrusion. In my early drafts, I use a lot of "telling" words too, but I try to weed them out completely before my final draft. Once you start noticing them, they are easy to spot, and it becomes easier to stay in Deep POV by revising your narrative.

Deeper POV is vital to good storytelling.

This method immerses the reader so deeply in the character's skin that any external narrator simply disappears. That is, the scene is not only told from that character's perspective, but it exemplifies the character's thoughts, emotions and reactions. In other words, it's the ultimate way to *show*, not tell.

I realize that some "telling" words are mandatory in narrative, but not when you are describing the character's thoughts, emotions, or attitudes. Those should all be shown by using the Deep POV technique.

It's natural to include filter words in your early drafts. However, before you self-publish, send your manuscript off to literary agents, or post any of your short stories, you should always go back through your manuscript and revise as many filter "telling" words as you can.

By adding detailed descriptions of characters' emotions, thoughts, and actions, it will help the reader imagine the sights, sounds, smells, and textures of each scene, allowing you to take your writing to the next level.

Don't let filter words clog your prose—describe the emotion!

We feel emotions; however, we use expressions to show them. When you are furious, your face gets hot and your voice rises to a higher pitch. That is how people around you know that you are enraged.

You don't tell them: "Watch it. I am so mad!" No, you display it through actions, gestures, and body language. That's how real people behave.

Narrative distance also puts extra words in your sentences, which aren't needed. So, try to cut out all of those pesky "telling" and shallow words that describe emotions such as: *love, hate, joy, grief, sorrow, sympathy, trepidation, fear, anger, irritation, hope, etc.* They can creep into your writing and weigh down your prose.

Never overuse rhetorical questions to show character emotion or confusion.

Often when a writer wants to express some kind of emotion like confusion in their characters, they will invoke a plaintive rhetorical question. While rhetorical questions can raise tension, only use them if necessary when you need to create Deep POV and cannot describe the reaction any other way. Remember as you revise that some rhetorical questions are fine, but *not* when used in abundance.

***

Over the course of this manual, I provide tons of examples from my own published novels and short stories to help you understand how to incorporate this amazing technique. Hopefully, they should spark your own creative muse and give you clever ideas on how to rewrite your shallow scenes.

Please take all of these suggestions to heart, and only make the changes that you feel will best suit your writing style and story.

SHALLOW WRITING

Deep POV is getting your reader so deeply submerged within the head of your characters that they experience—*really experience*—what the character is feeling. Don't just give readers a weak description—grab them by the throat and make them *feel* it.

One way to stay in close and personal (*show*, don't *tell*) is to do this: try to reduce as many filtering references as you can from your writing.

Instead, simply *show* us what the main character felt and saw and heard and decided, without using any overused "telling" phrases.

If a writer overuses filtering words that clutter up each sentence and remove the reader from the experience the character is undergoing or feeling, it creates narrative distance. Anything that describes the narrator's thought or mode of perception is considered "telling" the reader. If you can revise those sentences as much as possible, the POV will feel deeper and your prose will be greatly enhanced.

Also, if a critique partner or beta reader comments on something that confused them over the emotional reaction of one of your characters, check to make sure the stimulus cause is obvious to the reader through Deep POV. I advise to always try to include some type of an emotional response and a physical reaction to intensify the moment of any scene. This helps to *show* the character's response to what is happening by using the Deep POV method.

***

To really help you understand what Deep POV is and why it will turn your novel into an unputdownable read, I have compiled examples from my own published novels.

This excerpt was taken from the second book in my popular Spellbound series, SHATTERED SILENCE, to offer an example of how to use this wonderful technique. This first example is shallow writing and crammed with "telling" words. The second version is written in Deep POV, but it does contain only one or two filter words for better flow. The filter words are underlined.

Now compare the two illustrations below.

SHALLOW:

I could <u>feel</u> my head throbbing, which <u>made</u> me reluctant to open my eyes. I <u>could tell</u> that my vision was blurry. I took deep breaths because I <u>felt</u> dizzy and I <u>knew</u> I wasn't strong enough to raise my head. I leaned on one elbow. My tongue <u>felt</u> like it was glued to the roof of my mouth.

A door opened, and I <u>saw</u> a tall woman, with short red hair, wearing dark blue scrubs and clogs. She was tough looking like a man, I <u>thought</u>.

"You're awake. I'm Nurse Gwen. Let me fetch the doctor." She turned around and closed the door, then locked it.

Collapsing on the thin mattress, I <u>looked around</u> at my foreign surroundings. I <u>noticed</u> stark white walls, a metal-framed bed, and a nightstand. <u>There was</u> a solitary window with security wiring. I <u>heard</u> a loudspeaker call out codes and someone yelled. I <u>saw</u> a fluorescent light near the ceiling. I <u>could smell</u> bleach from the bedding and the antiseptic scent <u>made</u> me <u>feel</u> nausea.

I have no memory of how I'd gotten here, I <u>thought</u>.

There were no shadows on the walls. But eventually I <u>knew</u> they'd come for me. I <u>felt like</u> I had no protection here. I <u>felt</u> weak and <u>scared</u>.

I pulled off the sheets, and swung my legs over the bed. I was dressed in a hospital gown that <u>felt</u> scratchy and I had a bandage wrapped around my right wrist. I <u>noticed</u> that I had scrapes and bruises on my arms and legs. I could <u>see</u> a puncture wound on my arm where someone inserted a needle.

I <u>decided</u> to raise one hand to touch the gauze at my temple and <u>noticed</u> a white band on my left wrist: *Valley Grove Psychiatric Hospital: Trudell, Shiloh*

I <u>knew</u> then that I was in the hospital.

DEEP POV:

My head throbbed and I was reluctant to open my eyes. My vision blurry. I took deep breaths until the waves of dizziness lessened and I was strong enough to raise my head. I leaned on one elbow. My tongue felt glued to the roof of my mouth.

A door opened, admitting a tall lady—at least six feet—with short fiery-red hair, wearing dark blue scrubs and clogs. She looked tough and very butch. Bet nobody messed with her.

"You're awake. I'm Nurse Gwen. Let me fetch the doctor." She whipped around and closed the door. Locked it.

Collapsing on the thin mattress, I surveyed my foreign surroundings. Stark white walls, a metal-framed bed, and a nightstand. Solitary window with security wiring. Somewhere a loudspeaker called out codes and someone howled loudly. Fluorescent light glared down from the ceiling. Whiffs of bleach wafted from the bedding and the antiseptic scent gave me nausea.

I had no memory of how I'd gotten here.

No shadows danced on the walls. But eventually they'd come for me. I had no protection here. I was weak. Defenseless. Vulnerable.

I yanked off the crisp sheets, and swung my legs over the cold metal bed. Someone had dressed me in a scratchy hospital gown and wrapped my right wrist in an elastic Ace bandage. I had scrapes and bruises on my arms and legs. My forearm had a puncture wound where someone had inserted a needle. I raised one hand to touch the gauze at my temple and gasped at the band on my left wrist that read: *Valley Grove Psychiatric Hospital: Trudell, Shiloh*

Oh, no! I was in the nut house!

***

Remember that these are just "guidelines" to help improve your skills as a writer. Occasionally breaking the 'rules' is what a story calls for. But don't do it too often. By trying to create meaningful, descriptive prose, it will naturally move the story forward and convey a richer experience for your reader. Don't weigh it down with filter words.

I'm assuming that since you purchased this handbook, it's because you want to improve your writing skills. If you use the Deep POV technique, I promise that you'll notice an amazing difference in your writing. And I bet your readers will, too!

SHOW vs. TELL

So now you've written a remarkable story, revised your opener based on the great examples and advice from my other books, and had your manuscript critiqued by your critique partners, and read by beta readers…but is it ready?

First, ask yourself:

What are some of the generally overlooked mistakes writers make that send red flags to agents and publishers that their work isn't polished?

What common mistakes do many self-published writers make that instantly turn readers off?

Even an experienced writer and editor like myself always needs to triple-check my work before sending it out into the world. I continuously need to go back and revise all those annoying filter words.

For example, readers need details. They need to know the thoughts, feelings, and reactions to every occurrence. Instead of *telling* readers what those reactions and actions are, I would just let the reader figure it out for themselves. Readers need to smell the flowers, taste the apple, experience the fear, and feel the silky fabric of a dress. Anything less than that cheats the reader from deeply experiencing our fictional world.

Examine these two examples. The first is written in Shallow POV and the second is revised into Deeper POV and includes a few of the five senses and "voice" to bring the scene to life.

SHALLOW:

Simone saw the zombie shamble through the doorway. It had green drool coming from its mouth and the sight made Simone feel sick. The bad smell coming from the zombie's body caused her to cover her mouth and nose. She looked around for a weapon. She didn't notice anything handy, and realized that she was about to be attacked. She swallowed a frustrated scream.

DEEP POV:

The zombie shambled into the room. Toxic green saliva dripped from its mouth and she backed up. A sickly putrid stench of decay rose from the drooling brain-muncher. Simone almost gagged, pinching her nose with one hand. Her gaze quickly scanned the space. No guns. No real weapons. *This is not good!* Her heart rate tripled. She grabbed a baseball bat from the closet and faced the walking dead. *Game on.*

***

When a writer doesn't use Deep POV, it is called "telling." Most new writers use shallow writing, because they are not applying the Deep POV method.

A few common "telling" words include: *considered, regarded, wondered, saw, heard, hoped, realized, smelled, watched, touched, felt,* and *decided.*

These types of weak words are often used when the author wants to inform the reader of the character's reactions or emotions, rather than describing them directly. "Telling" is a method of expressing facts to the reader, but it is usually the *incorrect* way. In this handbook, I offer some practical ways to identify "telling" words and phrases.

***

Here is an excerpt taken from my novel LOST IN STARLIGHT that shows how using Deep POV correctly will enhance any scene.

DEEP POV:

Hayden glances in my direction and his extraordinary eyes lock onto mine. An unfamiliar thrill shoots through my veins. Even from a short distance, the boy looks mouthwatering good. His eyes harden into chips of ice.

Although I'm obviously busted, I can't look away. For a second, his gaze flares into the hottest flame. As though ignited by kerosene, my body temperature rises. There's a wariness lingering in his expression that I don't understand. Frightened and intrigued all at once, I tear my gaze away and a fierce spark of panic hits hard. Is my hair tangled? My pencil skirt unzipped? Lip gloss on my teeth?

Pulling a quick ninja hair check, I look out the nearby window, surreptitiously using the reflection to ensure that my flyaway hair looks tame. I sweep a hand around my waist to check my zipper and run my tongue over my teeth. All good. I grip the hem of my black tee under my leather jacket, the silver studded leather cuff on my wrist digging into my stomach, and yank it down. Much better.

Possibly embarrassing situation averted.

***

Did you grasp how I stay in Deep POV throughout that scene? Great!

The right way is to "show" by revealing information through action, dialogue, and the five senses like in the example above. Don't let weak filter words distance your writing. Most of these words can be deleted, and by using Deep POV instead, it will give your writing greater impact. Learn to be ruthless and revise those shallow sentences.

INFO-DUMPS

An info-dump can be a way of "telling" a reader, instead of describing it. As you revise your novel instead of stating the emotion for the reader, resulting in long passages of exposition, try to add some action, emotion, and reaction. Make use of the five senses: hearing, sight, touch, smell, and taste. Try to include descriptive words and Deep POV to enhance everything you write. You don't have to use each sense in every scene; one or two in any given situation will transform an otherwise tedious scene into a tangible and vivid experience for your reader.

Plus, "telling" the reader everything the character thinks or feels is boring and not needed. Instead, try to *show* by using Deep POV, which can and will enrich your story.

The filter "telling" words are underlined.

SHALLOW:

Jennifer _entered_ her bedroom and frowned. She _smelled_ her best friend's perfume and her husband's cologne. She _felt_ angry. She _decided_ that he must have been cheating on her.

DEEP POV:

Jennifer walked into her bedroom, planning to surprise her husband with a ten year anniversary gift. She stopped short and raised a trembling hand to her chest. *Oh, god. No!*

Her stomach lurched. The faint trace of her best friend's perfume lingered in the air, mingled with the musk scent of Jack's aftershave. *That lying, cheating jerk!*

***

Using Deeper POV will heighten every scene in your story and make your dialogue come to life.

This next example was taken from my novel SHATTERED SILENCE. Again, the shallower words are underlined.

SHALLOW (before revision):

Just when I thought my night couldn't possibly get any stranger...

I felt pain hurting the scar on my forearm. It burned. I felt tremors throughout my body. The mark began to vibrate and felt feverish. I slightly screamed in pain.

My dad and my aunt Lauren, standing beside me, instantly became concerned.

Dad rubbed my back. "Honey bunch, are you okay?"

I <u>knew</u> I couldn't talk, but I could nod. Something bad was here. I <u>knew</u> it.

"Relax, Shiloh. Just breathe," Aunt Lauren said. "Do you feel sick?"

I <u>heard</u> the doorbell chime.

I took a step back, bumping an end table. A vase fell over onto the floor. I <u>felt</u> an unnerving expectancy in the room. I felt like I was being smothered.

I <u>watched</u> Aunt Lauren bend down to pick up the vase. I <u>saw</u> my mother—Darrah—cross the room to answer the door.

I was <u>scared</u>. I <u>knew</u> something bad was ringing the doorbell. I <u>felt</u> like screaming and telling my mother, no.

***

This revised version written in Deeper POV *shows* the different emotions that the character is experiencing in this short scene.

Deep POV (after revision):

Just when I thought my night couldn't possibly get any stranger…

Pain pulsed across the jagged scar on my forearm. My mark burned, sharp and quick, like it did whenever something dangerous was around. My chest hurt. Tremors raked my limbs. The mark on my forearm vibrated and became feverish. A short scream tore from my lips.

My dad and my aunt Lauren, standing beside me, instantly became concerned.

Dad rubbed my back. "Honey bunch, are you okay?"

I couldn't speak, only nod. Something bad was here. I knew it in my bones.

"Relax, Shiloh. Just breathe," Aunt Lauren said. "Do you feel sick?"

The doorbell chimed.

Little pig, little pig, please, let me come in…

I took a step back, bumping an end table. A vase crashed to the floor. The room brimmed with an unnerving expectancy. I felt smothered, like I was crammed into a dangerous and airless place.

Aunt Lauren bent down to pick up the shards of porcelain from the vase. My mother—Darrah—crossed the room to answer the door.

Oh, god. It was here. Now. Ringing my damn doorbell.

I wanted to scream, *No! Don't open that door!*

***

I hope these examples help you to revise your own story into a gripping read!

INTROSPECTION

Inner-monologue or internal exposition is one of the essential ingredients used to create a comprehensive story. Unfortunately, it's all too often one of the most misused elements in story-telling. Since internal-monologue is slower and can be boring for the reader, find ways to bring it to life through Deep POV. Don't let your character's mental babble (long blocks of intro-spection) go on for pages at a time without a break by either dialogue or action.

Dialogue illustrates characterization quicker than any amount of exposition. If you disrupt the action and dialogue to include colossal chunks of description or introspection, it will remove the reader from the story.

Try to start each scene with a compelling bit of action, dialogue, and intrigue. Once the reader is "hooked," then go ahead and add in the necessary exposition.

Too much introspection or shallow writing can hinder the flow of the scene and smack of author intrusion by yanking the reader out of the story.

It is so much more powerful to be *shown* rather than *told* a character's thoughts, decisions, reactions, and feelings. In active scenes, interior monologue is also a powerful tool to make scenes more emotional and cause your dialogue to sparkle. Internal dialogue is a very effective technique, but one that should be used sparingly.

In almost every scene, I think it's important to stay in Deep POV. One way is to try to reduce the number of filtering references.

So rather than: "he/she think or thought," or "he/she felt, he/she see or saw," or "he/she hear or heard," or "he/she noticed," or "he/she realized," or "he/she wondered," or "he/she decided," or even "he/she wished," simply describe the emotion or thought or feeling through Deep POV.

Examples of weak "telling" words are underlined, along with examples on how to revise your sentences into Deep POV.

SHALLOW: I thought Tom was being a jerk.

DEEP POV: Tom was acting like a major jerkwad!

SHALLOW: Sammy felt the floor shake.

DEEP POV: The floor shook violently beneath Sammy's feet.

SHALLOW: Katie realized that she had forgotten her keys.

DEEP POV: *Oh, no!* Where did she leave her keys?

SHALLOW: I saw the cat pounce on the mouse.

DEEP POV: The cat crouched, tail swishing. Then the feline pounced on the unsuspecting mouse.

SHALLOW: Reed <u>heard</u> her mom's car pull into the driveway.

DEEP POV: Reed's ears perked up at the crunch of tires on the driveway.

SHALLOW: I <u>noticed</u> that Zander was angry.

DEEP POV: Zander's face reddened and he balled up his fist. *Ah, crud.*

SHALLOW: Sharon <u>wondered</u> if her daughter, Jill had passed her history test.

DEEP POV: Sharon frowned. *I sure hope Jill aces that test!*

SHALLOW: I <u>decided</u> to confront Zach during lunch.

DEEP POV: Instead of going to my usual table at lunch, I bypass my friends and their curious stares and storm right up to Zach.

SHALLOW: Max <u>wished</u> for a new bike more than anything for his birthday.

DEEP POV: Max put the ad for the bike in his mother's cookbook. That should be a clear hint!

***

I realize that you cannot remove every occurrence, but you can revise filter words and shallow writing most of the time. Just remember that Deep POV respects the reader's intelligence. Shallow writing presumes that your reader isn't clever enough to understand unless the writer states the emotion. But if you use the Deep POV method, it will immerse the reader into the story and induce an emotional response, which gives them a much deeper reading experience.

Another way to really use Deep POV effectively is to give each of your characters a distinctive "voice" that comes across in your narrative. Choose your words carefully, because they will reveal a lot about your character and vividly *show* their unique voice.

Look at these two examples from my published novel, IMMORTAL ECLIPSE:

SHALLOW (no voice):

I looked at the cream envelope on the kitchen table. I'd first thought that it was a wedding invitation. I hated being unmarried and having people give me a hard time about it. I didn't understand why being single and in my late twenties made my married friends give me odd looks. I was just independent.

DEEP POV:

My gaze rests on the cream envelope lying on the kitchen table. The one I'd first thought was a wedding invitation. Yet another nail in my unmarried-still-tragically-single coffin. Why does being single equate to being tossed in the bargain bin at Target? I'm a sophisticated and independent New Yorker, dammit!

***

Each sentence portrays the same scenario, but how the character reacts and is *shown* in the wording used to convey her thoughts and feelings is vastly different and gives the reader a Deeper POV. The first one is "telling" the reader info in a weak shallow way, but in the second version, we get a glimpse of her personality and "voice" and it is written in Deep POV.

To avoid "telling" words, a useful tool to help search out and eliminate repetitive or unproductive words is the FIND and REPLACE function in Microsoft Word. Either delete the weak word entirely or revise the sentence into actively showing. Alternatively, print the page and use a colored highlighter to single out needless words, and then re-edit the scene.

Just remember that you should always strive to *show* the emotion instead of telling the reader. The next few chapters will cover this in more detail with some great examples on how to revise your prose into Deeper POV.

In the subsequent chapters, I have listed tons of helpful examples of shallow filter words that you should try to revise. All of the Deep POV examples in this handbook have already been used in my published books or short stories, so you'll need to come up with your unique variations.

SHALLOW: FELT

In my opinion, *felt / feel* is the weakest word there is to describe an emotional reaction to something. In this chapter, I will show you examples on how to eliminate the biggest "telling" offender: *felt / feel / feeling / feels* from your writing, and how to transform the sentences below into vivid sensory details by using the Deep POV method.

Writing "I felt" or "He had a feeling" or "It feels so soft" or "I feel angry" is almost never necessary in Deeper POV. Instead of saying "he/she felt" something, simply describe the emotion instead. So I strongly encourage you to revise as many occurrences of the word *felt* as you can in your own manuscript before self-publishing, posting an online story, or sending your work off to a literary agent or publishing editor. You cannot remove them all, but any shallow writing that directly describes an emotion *can* be revised.

Eliminate these filter words: FELT / FEEL

SHALLOW: I <u>felt</u> a hand slap me sharply across the face.

DEEP POV: My head snapped back from the hard slap, my cheeks stinging from the unexpected blow.

SHALLOW: I <u>felt</u> angry, suddenly.

DEEP POV: Flaring my nostrils, I stomped forward and got right in Missy's face.

SHALLOW: He <u>felt</u> queasy.

DEEP POV: His stomach lurched, his breakfast threatening to cough back up.

SHALLOW: Charles <u>felt</u> his cheeks go red.

DEEP POV: Charles' cheeks heated, a red stain coloring his face.

SHALLOW: Tom <u>feels</u> a strong flare of jealousy.

DEEP POV: Tom stares hard at his best friend and the girl he's crushing on. His hands curl into fists at his sides, itching to swing out and put a dent in the wall beside him. *She's my girl!*

SHALLOW: He <u>felt</u> as though the top of his head would explode.

DEEP POV: His head pounded and his thoughts swirled.

SHALLOW: Jack <u>feels</u> unsteady on his feet.

DEEP POV: Jack wobbles forward, his legs unsteady.

SHALLOW: Mary <u>felt</u> a tightening in her stomach.

DEEP POV: Mary's stomach tightened.

SHALLOW: Scott <u>felt</u> his chest go tight.

DEEP POV: A deep ache snapped through him.

SHALLOW: Her heart <u>feels</u> as if it had just flopped over inside her ribcage.

DEEP POV: Her heart flops over inside her ribcage.

SHALLOW: She <u>felt</u> drowsy.

DEEP POV: Unable to stifle a yawn, she pulled up the blankets and closed her eyes.

SHALLOW: Lisa <u>felt</u> so disappointed and mad.

DEEP POV: Lisa's bottom lip trembled. She kicked at the ground with her sneaker. *This sucks!*

***

FELT / FEEL are filter words that will convey obvious information, while neatly inserting the dreaded narrative distance. The fact that the character *felt* whatever happens is understood by the reader without being told.

SHALLOW:

Max felt a flare of jealousy when he noticed his ex-girlfriend, Tammi with the new guy at work. Then he calmed down a little, deciding Tammi wasn't worth wasting his time.

He took a breath and pulled on his suit jacket. Then he looked over again and saw them kissing near the front counter.

Max felt so enraged that he felt his body tense up. The rage in his heart felt like it would explode. He moved closer to the office window and felt like he wanted to kill that guy.

He watched the new employee hitting on his girlfriend. Max knew Tammi belonged to him.

DEEP POV:

Max's mouth dropped open at the sight of ex-girlfriend, Tammi, flirting with the new guy at work. Heat boiled his insides. Then he relaxed his shoulders and blew out a breath.

Calm yourself, Max. She isn't worth wasting your time.

He tugged on his jacket, preparing to sell more cars today then the dirtbag chatting up his ex. But when he glanced over at them again, his chest tightened. The new guy had his tongue down Tammi's throat near the receptionist's desk. At work. In front of everybody.

Eyes narrowed and nostrils flared, he stomped closer to the office window to glare at them through the glass. Every muscle in his body tensed up.

Tammi's my girl! That new dude was gonna be nothing more than an oil stain when he was done plummeting him into the ground.

***

After reading the two different examples, could you see how *naming the emotion* and using "telling" words creates narrative distance?

The second example is a perfect illustration on how to describe a character's emotional state without *naming* the feeling.

SHALLOW: SEE

Always strive to revise shallow writing into Deep POV. Words like *see / saw / watch / could see* in a sentence "tell" the reader what the character is seeing or watching, instead of just describing it.

Eliminate these filter words: SAW / SEE

SHALLOW: I <u>see</u> the moon lift overhead.

DEEP POV: The moon hung in an inky sky overhead.

SHALLOW: He <u>saw</u> things moving, shifting.

DEEP POV: Things were moving, shifting.

SHALLOW: He <u>saw</u> nothing that threatened danger.

DEEP POV: He sensed nothing that threatened danger.

SHALLOW: She <u>saw</u> something out a window.

DEEP POV: Moving closer to the window, she peered through the glass.

SHALLOW: He <u>sees</u> the blue glow of the stars, and a milky ring around the moon.

DEEP POV: Glancing upward, he stares at the blue glow of the stars, and a milky ring around the moon.

SHALLOW: Sarah <u>saw</u> that he was wearing a black ski mask.

DEEP POV: Sarah stumbled back when he stepped forward wearing a black ski mask.

SHALLOW: He <u>sees</u> her sleek body moving through the water.

DEEP POV: He admires her sleek body moving through the water.

SHALLOW: I <u>could see</u> glints of gold in his blond hair.

DEEP POV: Glints of gold shone in his blond hair.

Eliminate these filter words: WATCH

SHALLOW: He <u>watched</u> the bird bobbing its head up and down.

DEEP POV: The bird was bobbing its head up and down.

SHALLOW: He <u>watched</u> as she walked back into the kitchen.

DEEP POV: She walked back into the kitchen, her hips swaying, and he smiled faintly to himself.

SHALLOW: I <u>watched</u> my father walk into the motel.

DEEP POV: I moved out of the way as my father strode into the motel.

SHALLOW: He <u>saw</u> Melanie put the lipstick into her purse and head out of the store.

DEEP POV: Glancing down the aisle, his eyes popped wide. Melanie slipped the lipstick into her bag, and then walked out of the store.

SHALLOW: Cary <u>watched</u> her car drive away and <u>felt his heart</u> sink in his chest.

DEEP POV: Cary stayed on the porch as she drove away, his heart sinking lower in his chest.

SHALLOW: Maggie <u>could see</u> the snowcapped mountains from the window of her hotel room.

DEEP POV: Throwing back the curtains, Maggie had a clear view of the snowcapped mountains from the window of her hotel room.

***

Effective Deep POV requires that you take your readers through the emotional experiences of your character as your character actually experiences them.

Using filter words like *watched / see / saw* only distances your reader and takes you out of Deeper POV, which is not what you want.

Again, let's use another example in order to clarify what I mean. Here's a snippet from my wildly popular novel LOST IN STARLIGHT, before revision (shallow) and after revising with the Deep POV technique. The heroine is writing a story for the school paper on a new guy at school, and she is confused by her attraction to him.

Please compare the two examples.

SHALLOW:

When my last class ends, I go to my locker to get my Trig textbook. I <u>hear</u> the doors at the end of the hall bang open, releasing students for the day and I <u>feel</u> it letting in a gust of air. I <u>notice</u> obtrusive fluorescent lights flicker overhead.

Across the hallway and a few lockers over from mine, I <u>can see</u> Zach and Hayden. I <u>look</u> at a red spray-painted slash on the metal door. I <u>decide</u> that someone must've spray painted Hayden's locker again.

While opening my locker, I <u>notice</u> Hayden's blatantly staring at me. I <u>discern</u> that he is taller than most boys.

I can <u>see</u> he has a messenger bag in one hand, and I <u>notice</u> drumsticks in his back pocket. I lift my hand to wave.

As I <u>watch</u> him, he doesn't return my gesture. He just continues gazing at me with unique eyes. I <u>feel</u> my head go woozy. It even <u>makes</u> my limbs <u>feel</u> jittery. Frustration and confusion are warring inside me for having *any* feelings whatsoever for someone like him. And I <u>wonder</u> why he is staring.

I feel a wave of nervousness because he is watching me. I wonder if there is something wrong. From the corner of my eye, I see him lean into the wall.

I think Hayden's stare is unsettling. I know there's something about that guy's rare smiles that draw girls to him. I decide that no one can resist Hayden Lancaster. Maybe not even me.

I see him watching me, and I feel heat on my skin. I notice Hayden isn't looking at my chest like most boys, which I know will only complicate my feelings for this boy.

DEEP POV:

When my last class ends, I stop at my locker to get my Trig textbook. The doors at the end of the hall bang open, releasing students for the day and letting in a gust of warm air. Several obtrusive fluorescent lights flicker overhead.

Across the hallway and a few lockers over from mine are Zach and Hayden. An angry red spray-painted slash taints the metal door. Some jerk must've tagged Hayden's locker again.

While opening my own locker, I'm suddenly aware that Hayden's blatantly staring at me. Hard to miss. He's like a man among boys, at least in his flawless physique. His messenger bag is in one hand, and drumsticks stick out of his back pocket.

I lift my hand in a hesitant little wave. He doesn't return my gesture, just continues gazing at me through those thick lashes that frame his unique eyes. My head goes all woozy. Even my limbs feel jittery. Frustration and confusion are warring inside me for having *any* feelings whatsoever for someone like him. And what's with the stare?

A wave of nervousness hits hard. Is there toilet paper hanging out of my jeans? Food stuck in my teeth? Or have Frankenstein bolts suddenly sprouted from my neck?

Being on Hayden's radar is a little unsettling. I admit there's something about Mr. Puppy Hero's rare smiles, lopsided with an edge, that draw girls to him like insects buzzing a bug zapper. For better or worse, no one can resist Hayden Lancaster. Not even me.

Our gazes lock for just one second, and heat rushes beneath my skin. Hayden isn't gawking at my chest like most boys. He's only looking at my face, which further complicates my feelings for this strange guy.

***

So from the first shallow example, you can see that those extra "telling" words will clog up your sentence structure and remove your reader from Deeper POV. In the second example, I left only one "telling" word for better flow.

Once you start applying Deep POV to your own writing, you'll know that there are times to use a "tell" word if it reads awkwardly when omitted.

SHALLOW: HEARD

A very common "telling" word is *heard / hear*, which instantly takes a writer out of Deeper POV. If your reader already knows in whose POV the scene is written, why would you need to explain what he/she is hearing?

Eliminate these filter words: HEAR / HEARD

SHALLOW: I hear a scream from the kitchen—it sounds like Amy is scared.

DEEP POV: An earsplitting scream echoes through the house. I guess Amy must've seen Michael's ghost.

SHALLOW: She heard the sound of the car coming.

DEEP POV: The Ford's tires screeched, kicking up gravel on the road.

SHALLOW: Kate could hear the crackling of burning wood.

DEEP POV: The burning wood crackled and spit.

SHALLOW: She <u>heard</u> a strange whoosh <u>sound</u> and looked up.

DEEP POV: A strange *whooshing* came from overhead.

SHALLOW: He <u>heard</u> the stubbornness in her tone of voice.

DEEP POV: There was a distinct stubbornness in her tone of voice.

SHALLOW: They <u>heard</u> another scream, high-pitched and frightened.

DEEP POV: Another high-pitched scream echoed throughout the woods.

SHALLOW: He could <u>hear</u> the roaring of his own pulse.

DEEP POV: His pulse roared in his ears.

SHALLOW: She <u>heard</u> the howl of a wolf.

DEEP POV: The lonely howl of a wolf resonated in the night air.

SHALLOW: I <u>heard</u> the sob in his voice.

DEEP POV: His words faded, but the sob in his voice remained.

SHALLOW: Everyone looked at the field when they <u>heard</u> the whistle blow.

DEEP POV: The game was about to start. When the whistle blew, everyone looked at the field.

SHALLOW: We heard the thunder rumble in the distance.

DEEP POV: Thunder rumbled in the distance.

SHALLOW: I heard the bedroom door slam down the hall.

DEEP POV: The bedroom door down the hall slammed shut.

SHALLOW: Ian heard the soft murmur of voices.

DEEP POV: The soft murmur of voices reached Ian's keen ears.

***

I have included another excerpt from the fourth book in my YA series, RECKLESS REVENGE, which will give you an idea on how to eliminate *hear / heard* filter words from your own writing. The first example has very little "voice" and too many shallow sentences that clutter the narrative and distance the reader.

SHALLOW:

For a moment I thought about casting a spell that would illuminate the yard, but I decided not to. I forced my fingers away from the gemstone and took a deep breath.

Until I heard loud howls from the woods. I didn't think it was coyotes or wolves. I knew this was Northern California. Then I thought that maybe I *should* use my witchy superpowers.

I felt the hairs on the back of my neck stand up. But I decided to stay there on purpose to test myself. I hated letting fear get the better of me.

The night air felt cold and crisp. I could hear the weeping willow tree sway in the breeze. Beyond the back fence, I could see the forest with giant redwoods that soared to heights that seemed to touch the clouds.

Staring into the utter darkness, I felt my palms grow damp. As I watched, every shadow seemed to shift and stretch.

Maybe it was just my fear of the dark, but I felt that fight-or-flight response kick in. Maybe I should run into the house and lock the door.

I heard another howl come out of the forest, and I felt my skin crawl with gooseflesh on my arms.

I knew something nasty was roaming the woods, something angry and loud. I decided to back up while watching the yard for any threats.

DEEP POV:

For a moment, I considered casting a spell that would illuminate the yard, but fought the urge. Forced my fingers away from the gemstone and breathed deeply.

Until chilling howls emanated from the woods. Not coyotes or wolves. This was Northern California. On second thought…maybe I *should* use my witchy superpowers.

The hairs on the back of my neck stood up. But I stayed there on purpose to test myself. I hated letting fear get the better of me. And because I was a control junkie, I had the profound desire to conquer all the things that frightened me...well, to a certain extent, anyway.

The night air was cold and crisp. The weeping willow tree swayed in the breeze, leaves falling from the branches like autumn rain. Beyond the back fence, the forest with giant redwoods—ancient trees, thousands of years old—soared to heights that seemed to touch the clouds. Staring into the utter darkness, I felt my palms grow damp. Every shadow seemed to shift and stretch.

Maybe it was just my fear of the dark, but that fight-or-flight response was kicking in, begging me to run into the house and lock the door. No, more like it was screaming: *Forget being all heroic and fearless and get your butt back inside!*

Another howl came out of the forest, and my skin crawled, ripples of gooseflesh prickling my arms.

Something nasty was roaming the woods, something angry and loud. I backed up toward the house, my gaze scanning the yard for threats.

***

Could you tell the difference in the two examples?

There is only one "telling" word in the second example, and even that word could be omitted, but was left for easier readability. Notice how closely we stay inside the heroine's head throughout the passage, except for that one *felt* verb in the paragraph when I go shallow for better sentence flow. Although, it is not describing an emotion, even that shallow sentence could be revised into Deeper POV.

SHALLOW: Staring into the utter darkness, I <u>felt</u> my palms grow damp.

DEEP POV: Staring into the utter darkness, my palms grew damp.

As you start to revise your own work, remember that it is easy to unintentionally violate the *show, don't tell* principle when you include filtering words into the narrative. But now I encourage you to weed them out.

SHALLOW: LOOKED

Decreasing the amount of filter words like "looked / appeared" from your writing will transform any narrative into Deeper POV. The object of Deep POV is to secure the reader inside the character's head without using shallower words that litter your prose and distance your reader.

Using "looked" or "appeared" to describe an object, setting or character expression is considered shallower writing. As an alternative, I would describe by *showing* the emotional reaction or the character's expression to keep your writing in Deeper POV.

Eliminate these filter words: LOOKED / APPEARED

SHALLOW: He looked angry.

DEEP POV: His eyes bulged and his lips pressed into a thin line.

SHALLOW: Ally looked at Scott in horror.

DEEP POV: Ally gazed at Scott, her big brown eyes wide.

SHALLOW: Misty <u>looked</u> so stricken.

DEEP POV: Misty wrung her hands and tears welled in her eyes.

SHALLOW: Lydia <u>looked</u> as if she hadn't slept at all.

DEEP POV: Lydia yawned and rubbed at her sleepy eyes.

SHALLOW: She <u>looked</u> less than thrilled.

DEEP POV: Her mouth pulled downwards into a pout.

SHALLOW: Darla huffed and <u>appeared</u> to mull over the offer.

DEEP POV: Darla huffed and tapped her chin as if mulling it over.

SHALLOW: The house <u>appeared</u> quiet, almost peaceful.

DEEP POV: The house was too quiet, almost peaceful.

SHALLOW: I <u>looked around</u> the park for David. (Overused "to view" word)

DEEP POV: My gaze swept the park for David. No sign of him on the swings or the slide.

SHALLOW: She <u>looked</u> contemplative.

DEEP POV: She puckered her lips and nodded.

SHALLOW: He <u>looked</u> at me, and I <u>looked</u> back. (Overused "to view" word)

DEEP POV: He gazed at me, and I stared back.

SHALLOW: Zayne <u>looked</u> really <u>mad</u>.

DEEP POV: Shaking a fist in the air, Zayne glared at Bobby.

SHALLOW: Monique was <u>looking</u> <u>amazed</u>.

DEEP POV: Monique's hand lifted to cover her heart and she squealed.

***

Writing Tip: Stating that a character "looks or looked" is a bland way to tell the reader that he/she is viewing or seeing something. It is overused, and in my opinion, it is nothing more than stage direction.

Did he/she *gaze, glare, peer, stare, study, glance, gawk, blink at, glower, frown,* or *gape*? Any of these convey more information to the reader.

***

Again, sometimes "look / looked" or "appear / appeared" is okay to use in a sentence if it improves flow and creates easier readability.

Here is another excerpt that will show you how to use the Deep POV technique and take your writing skills to the next level.

The excerpt was taken from my own published novel the first book in the Spellbound series, BEAUTIFULLY BROKEN. The heroine, Shiloh, is sitting in the car with her mother and they're parked in front of a spooky mansion

SHALLOW:

When the ghost floated away and dissolved, I looked at Darrah. I noticed her gaze was still fixated on Craven Manor. But Darrah's face changed in an instant. I opened my mouth to speak as I looked at her, but the hatred I saw twisting her features made me feel cold. Some old memory seemed to put a wry smile on her lips as I looked at her face, a smile, which appeared painted, suspended over skin. As I watched, she shimmered like an illusion, her expression looked both shrewd and ominous. Her face looked altered, as though her disguise had been removed. It appeared as if her aura thundered.

Her aura made me scoot away. Since my muddled suicide attempt, I could view auras. Looking at my mother now, I could see her aura flare with darker hues. This woman appeared angry and looked like someone else.

DEEP POV:

When the wraith floated away and dissolved within the fog, I glanced at Darrah. Her gaze was still fixated on Craven Manor. But Darrah's face changed in an instant. I opened my mouth to speak, but the hatred twisting her features stopped me cold. Her aura thundered, rolling off her flesh in icy waves. Some old memory seemed to put a wry smile on her lips, a smile which appeared painted, suspended over skin. She shimmered like an illusion, her expression both shrewd and ominous. Altered, as though her disguise had been removed, yet her flawless beauty flickered beneath.

Her aura had me scooting away. Since my muddled suicide attempt—when I'd almost died—I could see auras. Echoes of souls, which revealed a person's true nature, bound in colors that held meanings. Her aura flared with dark hues. She was not the same woman who'd raised me. This was *not* my mother. This was an ice queen.

***

From that last example, you can see that I only used one or two filter words for easier readability, but even they could be revised into Deeper POV to enhance the scene. Once you start noticing shallow writing, it will get much easier to revise your own manuscript.

SHALLOW: SOUND

This chapter will cover ways to eradicate filter words like *sounds / sound* from your writing that "tell" instead of "show." Below are some examples on how to help rewrite these offenders. In my opinion, the word "sound" is extensively overused in fiction.

Did the character hear a *noise, hum, echo, thud, reverberation, crash, jingle, clatter,* or *vibration*? Any of which are more specific for the reader.

Not all "telling" words can be completely removed from your prose. That would be difficult and cause some of your writing to become awkward. If including a filter word like "sounded" in the sentence creates easier readability and avoids passive writing, I would leave it.

Eliminate these filter words: SOUNDS / SOUND

SHALLOW: There was a <u>sound</u> in the bushes.

DEEP POV: The bushes rattled with a menacing shake.

SHALLOW: I <u>heard</u> the <u>sound</u> of his boots echoing off the floor.

DEEP POV: The heavy thud of his boots echoed off the floor.

SHALLOW: A <u>sound</u> from inside the pantry startled him.

DEEP POV: A *crash* came from inside the pantry, and he flinched.

SHALLOW: The <u>sound</u> of thunder made the house shudder.

DEEP POV: The boom of thunder shook the house.

SHALLOW: He jerked at the <u>sound</u> of his father's voice from the doorway.

DEEP POV: His father's loud voice seeped beneath the doorway and his body jerked.

SHALLOW: The <u>sound</u> of the siren had receded.

DEEP POV: The siren's wail receded.

SHALLOW: He began striding toward the <u>sounds</u> of chaos.

DEEP POV: He strode toward the uproar of chaos.

SHALLOW: The only <u>sounds</u> were the muted muffle of my footsteps.

DEEP POV: The muted muffle of my footsteps were the only detectable noises.

SHALLOW: The smallest sounds resonated throughout the empty house.

DEEP POV: Throughout the empty house, slight noises echoed.

SHALLOW: The only sound I could hear were the rhythmic pounding of blood in my eardrums.

DEEP POV: Everything was muffled except the rhythmic pounding of blood in my eardrums.

SHALLOW: The sound of beating wings was balm to his soul.

DEEP POV: The resonance of beating wings was balm to his soul.

SHALLOW: I heard the sound of the garage door open.

DEEP POV: The garage door whirred open.

***

Here is another example that illustrates how to revise Shallow POV into a much Deeper POV for your readers taken from one of my short stories.

The first example is before revision and has a lot "telling." The narrative is also cluttered with filter words, and does not have enough "voice." The second example is written close and personal (Deep POV), with a more emotional punch.

Please compare the two excerpts.

SHALLOW:

The sound of students loudly talking makes me irritated. I notice Kevin Wells squirming in his seat, looking angry. The kid next to me smells like stinky feet and unwashed hair, making me want to throw up.

As I search my purse for a pen, a weird sound has me looking around. I see the teacher run his fingernails down the chalkboard to get everyone's attention. Finally, I find an uncapped pen, but when I go to start the test, I see the ballpoint only writes a faded blue line. I try it again, but it doesn't work. All dried up, I thought.

Then I hear the sound of the warning bell as everybody finally takes their seats.

Feeling frustrated, I feel a tap on my shoulder. I decide to ignore it, but I feel the person tap my shoulder again.

"Hey," the boy asks. "Do you need a pen?"

I decide to turn around. It's the new guy from Bio class. I would have noticed the peculiar outfit—long coat, black boots—not to mention his blue eyes anywhere. He is close enough for me to touch if I want to. His eyes look so dark, they appear almost a black color. His eyeballs are looking at me with a frightening intensity. I feel my heart pounding, and feel frozen in my seat.

The sound of a book falling to the floor makes me flinch.

DEEP POV:

The students are making so much noise that I grind my teeth. My nerves are already frazzled from the pop quiz that Mr. Jenkins has sprung on us today.

Kevin Wells squirms in his seat, his ears bright red. Guess he isn't prepared for the test, either. The stench of stinky feet and unwashed hair comes from the boy across from me. My nose wrinkles and I try not to gag.

Ever hear of a shower, buddy?

As I dig through my purse for a pen, an ear-splitting noise echoes throughout the room. I want to cover my ears. The History teacher runs his fingernails down the chalkboard and instantly everyone quiets down.

My fingers touch an uncapped pen in my bag. *Whew!* But when I press the tip to the paper to write my name, the ballpoint only creates a faded blue line. I shake the pen and try again. Nada. Zilch. I slouch in my seat. Dang it.

The warning bell clangs loudly and everybody finally takes their seats.

Chewing my lip, I swallow hard. If I get up now and go to my locker, I'll get a tardy *and* might not have enough time to finish the quiz.

What should I do? Go or stay?

A hand taps my shoulder. I ignore it, but the person behind me taps harder. *Ouch!*

"Do you need a new pen?" someone whispers behind me.

I slowly turn around. It's that weirdly hot guy from Bio class. He's hard to miss, dressed in his usual outfit—black trench coat, scuffed combat boots—not to mention his strange eyes. He's sitting directly behind me. Near enough to touch. His dark eyes are almost black, and he gazes at me with an unnerving intensity. My heart races, and my butt feels glued to the seat.

Why is he staring at me like that? Like he can tell what I look like without my clothes on. I shudder, but I can't look away.

A textbook hits the floor with a resounding thud. My body jerks like a puppet and the noise breaks the spell.

***

The second example has rich details and uses the five senses. There are only one or two *shallow* words in that excerpt, and it has "voice" and action and emotion. Even though it is mostly straight exposition, the Deep POV technique pulls the reader deeper into the story.

SHALLOW: SMELL

This chapter covers how to revise "telling" words from your sentences by using the five senses and omitting the offending words *smell / smelled* from your prose to avoid narrative distance. For Deeper POV, certain distancing words should be removed from your story as much as possible. However, it is always okay to use shallow "telling" words in dialogue.

One way to write in Deep POV is by incorporating the senses, and "smell" is a natural reaction that can be included in almost every scene that you write. In Deeper POV, we experience what the character experiences. We smell the aromas, touch the same textures, and we experience the same emotions.

Eliminate these filter words: SMELL / SMELLED

SHALLOW: Suddenly he smelled smoke.

DEEP POV: Billows of smoke burned his nostrils.

SHALLOW: Her hair smelled really good.

DEEP POV: The heavenly scent of her hair—maybe roses—combined with the sunlight glittering on those gold strands caused his heart to thump.

SHALLOW: He <u>smelled</u> her perfume.

DEEP POV: The lingering trace of her flowery perfume invaded his senses.

SHALLOW: I can <u>smell</u> his clean, vital scent.

DEEP POV: His scent hits my nostrils, fresh linen and expensive body-wash.

SHALLOW: The room <u>smells</u> very clean when I go inside.

DEEP POV: The fragrance of leather, wood, and orange furniture polish surrounds me as I enter the room.

SHALLOW: I could <u>smell</u> his cloying sweet cologne.

DEEP POV: The nauseating stench of his aftershave made me want to gag.

SHALLOW: She <u>smelled</u> sweet, like strawberries or maybe peaches.

DEEP POV: A sweet aroma, like strawberries or peaches, wafted from her freshly washed hair.

SHALLOW: A thick sulfur <u>smell</u> was filling one corner of the gym.

DEEP POV: A thick sulfur odor filled one corner of the gym.

SHALLOW: He smelled like a campfire, and I buried my face in his chest.

DEEP POV: His skin and clothes held the scent of a campfire, and I hugged him close.

SHALLOW: The bedroom smelled of dust and thickness.

DEEP POV: The bedroom reeked of dust and a strange thickness.

***

Here is another example from one of my short stories. Try to avoid "telling" the reader how something *smelled / smells*.

SHALLOW:

Anne touched his shoulder and pointed with her nose. At first, Ryan couldn't figure out what she was trying to tell him.

Then he smelled it. The smell of gunpowder.

He headed toward the smell. He turned the corner down a dark alleyway—and saw his brother Peter lying on the ground with Nathan standing beside him.

Ryan and Anne hid behind a dumpster. The smell of rotting garage and old food made him feel sick. Ryan moved and took a quick look. Peter's aura was gone. He <u>appeared</u> dead. Nathan had murdered him.

DEEP POV:

Anne tapped his shoulder and jerked her chin, scrunching up her nose.

Ryan glanced at her with raised eyebrows. "What?" he whispered.

"Shhh," she replied quietly, putting a finger to her lips. "Do you smell that?"

Ryan shook his head, then the smoky odor of gunpowder filled the night air.

Sniffing, Ryan stamped in the direction of the offending stench. When he turned the corner down a dark alleyway—he halted in his tracks.

No, no, no!

His brother Peter lay on the ground in a pond of red with Nathan standing over him. A handgun rested in Nathan's closed fist. Sweat beaded his forehead. He did not look up.

Ryan and Anne quickly ducked behind a dumpster. The stink of rotting garage and decaying food wafted from inside and Ryan's stomach roiled.

This cannot be happening.

He leaned out and took another peek. Peter's aura gradually vanished. His brother was dead. And that evil jerk Nathan had murdered him.

***

Anytime that you can remove the sensory "tell" from your scenes and clearly state whatever it is the character *saw* or *felt* or *tasted* or *heard* or *smelled*, it will automatically put you into Deeper POV.

SHALLOW: KNEW

As you revise, keep in mind that Deep Point of View is only one of many techniques that writers can utilize to craft a story that takes their writing skills to the next level.

In this chapter, we will examine filter words like *know / knew* that can take writers out of Deep POV in order to gain a stronger understanding of the purpose and nature of this awesome technique.

Eliminate these filter words: KNEW / KNOW

SHALLOW: He knew his dad wasn't keeping up with the child support payments.

DEEP POV: His dad had stopped keeping up with the child support payments months ago.

SHALLOW: She sure knew how to kiss.

DEEP POV: *Wow.* His toes curled from the soft, erotic kiss.

SHALLOW: She <u>knew</u> he was lying.

DEEP POV: He glanced away when he told her he'd been at the office all day. A sure sign he was lying!

SHALLOW: I <u>know</u> Matt likes me a lot.

DEEP POV: The way Matt stares at me during Trig is an indication he wants more than friendship.

SHALLOW: Derek <u>knew</u> exactly how that would go down.

DEEP POV: Derek frowned. This would *not* go down well.

SHALLOW: When I touched his shoulder, I <u>knew</u> something was wrong.

DEEP POV: I touched his shoulder and he flinched as if something was wrong.

SHALLOW: I needed to <u>know</u> how awful my infraction was when it came to Thomas.

DEEP POV: Thomas might never forgive my infraction, but I had to find out.

SHALLOW: I <u>know</u> I haven't been a werewolf that long, but the full moon <u>makes</u> me twitchy.

DEEP POV: Although, I haven't been a werewolf for very long, my skin gets twitchy every full moon.

SHALLOW: I did not <u>know</u> who would come through that door.

DEEP POV: I had no idea who might come through that door.

SHALLOW: Shane <u>knew</u> his voice was low and <u>angry</u>, but he didn't care.

DEEP POV: Shane's voice was low and toxic, but he didn't care.

SHALLOW: I <u>knew</u> he wouldn't be in French class.

DEEP POV: The final bell rang, which meant he was ditching French class again today.

***

Here is another great example from the fifth book in my YA series, DESTINY DISRUPTED on how to avoid "telling" the reader that the character *knows / knew* something.

Read both examples and compare.

SHALLOW:

I <u>knew</u> it the second he walked into the room. Daniel, my boyfriend's best friend, was <u>mad</u> at me. I <u>knew</u> I couldn't really blame him after he'd caught me cheating on Trent. In my heart, I <u>knew</u> it was just one little kiss shared with a fallen angel and I'd regretted it the second it had happened. But I had to <u>know</u> if he told anyone about what he saw.

"You can't tell him, please," I said with a whine.

Daniel looked at me for a moment, then laughed. He chuckled and it was full of resentment.

"Okay, Shiloh," he said once he finished laughing. "But I have a request."

My heart felt sick. I knew what he thought of me now. "What?"

He looked thoughtful. "You can do my homework."

"I can do that," I said really fast.

We were both silent. I grimaced and looked around.

"I cannot believe you," he said, looking at me like I was a bad person. "You are not the same girl from last summer. But your secret is safe."

I felt tears on my face. I knew crying and begging would not work on Daniel. He was kind and levelheaded and the words hurt me. But at least I knew he would keep my secret. He was the most honest person I knew. However awful his tone sounded like, I knew the promise was just as strong.

Then he turned his back on me, and I knew he would always hate me.

DEEP POV:

My boyfriend's best friend, Daniel, strolled into the room and our eyes locked. His lips curled upward and his eyes became slits of hatred.

Oh, god. This is gonna be awkward.

He'd glimpsed me kissing that fallen angel, Raze last night, and I had to find out if he had told anyone yet. Mainly one person.

"You can't tell Trent, please," I begged. "It was a *huge*, really stupid mistake."

Daniel stared at me for a moment, then shook his head and laughed. He chuckled so bitterly, I'm not even sure the noise could be classified as a real laugh.

"Okay, Shiloh," he said finally, once his snickering quieted down. "On one condition."

My body relaxed a little, but my heart pinched. "Name it."

Daniel rubbed his chin and smirked. "Do my homework for a month."

"Fine. Anything," I said quickly and bit my quivering lip. "Just, please don't tell him. He's been going through so much lately. This would crush him."

An uncomfortable silence descended.

"Fine, but I seriously cannot believe you," he said, looking at me like I was lower than pool scum. "You're *not* the same girl I met last summer. But don't stress it—your slutty little secret is safe with me."

Tears spilled down my hot cheeks. Coming from Daniel—someone who was naturally so compassionate and even-tempered—the words and his ugly tone couldn't have stung more.

But he'd keep my secret. He was the most decent, honest guy on campus. However hurtful his wording was, the promise was forever.

"Look, Daniel—"

"Save it," he said with a sigh.

Then he turned his back on me, and my stomach dropped into my feet.

***

Most of us have heard the saying *"show, don't tell"* many times. In order for a reader to become deeply involved in a story, they must be able to visualize the setting, hear the sounds, imagine touching the objects, and even smell everything within the scene.

I sincerely hope these examples help you to revise your own stories into great reads.

SHALLOW: THOUGHT

Lessening the amount of direct thought sentences like *he/she thought* or *she/he told themselves* will only force your narrative into Deeper POV. Remember that the objective of conveying character emotion through Deep POV is to anchor the reader inside the character's head without mentioning her/his thoughts.

Eliminate this filter word: THOUGHT

SHALLOW: I'd better go to the store right after work, he thought.

DEEP POV: If Lacy was coming over for dinner, he'd better stop by the market after work.

SHALLOW: She was still thinking about the party and what went wrong.

DEEP POV: *The party was such a disaster!* Things could've gone smoother if she'd hired a DJ.

SHALLOW: Steven is such a jerk, she <u>thought</u> <u>angrily</u>.

DEEP POV: If Steven kept flirting with her best friend, he was gonna regret it!

SHALLOW: I <u>thought</u> that getting a promotion would solve all my problems.

DEEP POV: I sighed. That big promotion didn't help me financially liked I'd hoped.

SHALLOW: Maybe I should wear this green shirt today, <u>she</u> <u>thought</u>.

DEEP POV: Standing in the closet, she tugged a green blouse from the hanger. *This will go perfect with my new shoes.*

SHALLOW: Let him find out the hard way, she <u>thought</u>.

DEEP POV: She rolled her eyes. Her brother was so hard-headed sometimes.

SHALLOW: I <u>thought</u> I <u>saw</u> Danny cringe at the mention of his dad.

DEEP POV: Glancing over at Danny, I barely caught him cringe at the mention of his dad

SHALLOW: Except for the dragon tattoo on his chest, <u>she</u> <u>thought</u> with a smile.

DEEP POV: She smiled. Except for the dragon tattoo on his chest, he was unmarked.

SHALLOW: A terrifying <u>thought</u> occurred to me. (Cliché)

DEEP POV: My limbs shook and my pulse spiked. What if the killer came back before I escaped?

***

These next two examples show how to eliminate problems with shallow writing and how to revise the filter word *thought*.

SHALLOW:

Meg <u>thought</u> about what Evan had done. He could so easily lie about it, <u>she told herself</u>. And she almost <u>wished</u> he would lie, she <u>thought</u>, just so that she could walk away without any real heartache.

"Did you really kiss Carrie?" Meg asked, in a <u>jealous</u> tone. "Why would you do that?"

A smile crept over his face, and for a second she <u>thought</u> that he resembled the boy she once <u>knew</u> and loved before he broke her heart.

He shrugged. "Wouldn't you like to know. Sorry, but that's between Carrie and me."

Meg <u>felt</u> tears in her green eyes. "How could you do this to us?"

She never would've <u>thought</u> they'd end up this way—with her <u>feeling</u> so <u>bitter</u> and <u>dejected</u>.

DEEP POV:

Meg's face went deathly pale. She stared straight ahead, eyes fixed on Evan, as if begging him to tell her the truth.

Her stomach panged. *Maybe I don't want to know.* He might even lie about it. But that wasn't Evan's style.

"You kissed Carrie?" Meg's skin heated and warmth radiated from her pores. "*Why* would you do that?"

A smile touched his full lips, his usual smirk, and for a second he resembled the boy she once loved, before he'd met Carrie, before he'd broken her heart.

"Does it matter? We broke up two weeks ago, Meg." Evan shrugged and kicked at the ground with a dirty Converse. "Sorry, but that's between Carrie and me."

Tears sprang to Meg's green eyes. "How could you do this to us? I thought we were going to try and work things out."

"It's too late for that. I'm with Carrie now," he said coldly.

Meg's heart sank lower in her chest and sobs build up in her throat. *It can't end like this. It just can't!*

***

Did those examples spark your own creative muse? I hope so!

As you rewrite certain scenes where information is being revealed between characters, remember that they should still be moving, reacting, and *showing* emotion to keep the pace of the scene flowing smoothly.

SHALLOW: CAUSED

Another common issue with narrative distance is the tendency to try to convey emotional reactions through weaker sentence structures by using filtering words such as "made / making" or "caused / causing" which *tell* how the character reacts after something happens. If you use Deep POV instead, you'll avoid slipping into this kind of shallower "telling" style.

Do I use these filtering words on occasion? Yes, because I mostly write in first-person POV and sometimes they are hard to avoid without creating awkward sentences. However, my advice is this: if you can rewrite the sentence without it and stay in Deep POV, do it. If some of the time you cannot, then go ahead and leave the shallow word in the sentence.

Eliminate these filter words: MADE / CAUSED

SHALLOW: My heart pounded loudly and it <u>made</u> it hard to breathe.

DEEP POV: My heartbeat pounded in my chest. Now it was nearly impossible to breathe.

SHALLOW: "You look cute in pink," he teased, <u>making</u> me genuinely smile.

DEEP POV: "You look cute in pink," he teased, and the smile that lifted the corners of my mouth was genuine.

SHALLOW: The barking dog was <u>making</u> my stomach clench.

DEEP POV: My stomach clenched. When was that barking dog going to shut up?

SHALLOW: That condescending tone always <u>made</u> my teeth grind.

DEEP POV: Whenever he used that condescending tone, I gritted my teeth.

SHALLOW: Just the sight of him <u>made</u> my heart leap.

DEEP POV: My heart leaped at the sight him.

SHALLOW: When I dropped my ice cream cone, it <u>made</u> her cackle.

DEEP POV: The ice cream cone slipped from my fingers and hit the pavement. My friend took one look and cackled like a witch.

SHALLOW: A shiver rips up my spine <u>causing</u> every little body hair to stand up.

DEEP POV: A shiver zips up my spine, and every fine body hair stands on end.

SHALLOW: The close contact had <u>caused</u> a heat to rise deep inside her.

DEEP POV: He stood too close to her and heat rose deep inside her.

SHALLOW: The weight of <u>disappointment</u> <u>caused</u> Claire's shoulders to sag.

DEEP POV: Claire's shoulders sagged.   Losing the football game meant no after party. And no hooking up with the cute quarterback.

SHALLOW: He grips my hips harder, <u>causing</u> my joints to ache.

DEEP POV: His grip tightens on my hips and my joints ache at his rough touch.

SHALLOW: He glared at her with <u>hatred</u>, <u>causing</u> her heart to stutter.

DEEP POV: He glared at her as if at any second he would breathe fire out of his nostrils. Her heart stuttered and she took a step back.

SHALLOW: The bumpy bus ride <u>caused</u> her to drop her purse and the contents spilled out.

DEEP POV: The bus rumbled down the street, hitting every pothole. She was jostled from her seat, and the purse sitting in her lap tumbled to the dirty floor. *Just great.* The contents spilled everywhere, rolling and sliding in the aisle.

***

Just remind yourself as you revise that "telling" is shallow writing and means putting extra words into your sentence that remove the reader from the experience that the character is going through or feeling. Anything that describes the narrator's thought or mode of perception is considered "telling" the reader about whatever the characters are experiencing. And you're reminding the reader of the character's presence (author intrusion) by drawing attention to the fact that he/she is a character in a book that they're reading. If you can revise these sentences as much as possible, the point of view will feel deeper.

To be clear, I'm not saying that "telling" filter words should be completely eliminated from your manuscript. That would be impossible and make some of your prose become particularly awkward.

SHALLOW: DECIDED

In Deep POV, writers don't need to write *he/she decided* or *he/she considered*. These types of "telling" phrases are murder to Deep POV, because they smack of author intrusion. Readers are now distanced from the character, and they are not in their head where they belong.

Eliminate this filter word: DECIDED

SHALLOW: I decided to walk home instead of taking the bus.

DEEP POV: Walking home would give me some much needed exercise, *and* I'd avoid sitting next to Loud Mouth Simon on the bus.

SHALLOW: If he had decided on which girl to take the prom sooner, he wouldn't be dateless now.

DEEP POV: If he hadn't waited until the last minute to ask two different girls, he'd be having a blast at the prom right now.

SHALLOW: Maryann <u>heard</u> about the quiz in Trig and she <u>decided</u> to ditch class.

DEEP POV: From the classroom door, grunts and groans echoed off the walls. Maryann backed up into the hall. *Pop quiz?* No thanks.

SHALLOW: Lucas stared at the menu and <u>decided</u> on the turkey sandwich.

DEEP POV: Lucas's stomach rumbled while he scanned the menu. Hmmm, a turkey sandwich sure would quiet those hunger pangs.

SHALLOW: Lori <u>considered</u> dressing as a ghost for Halloween.

DEEP POV: Lori grabbed a white sheet from the closet. This would make an easy costume for the Halloween party. All it needed was two eyeholes.

SHALLOW: Amy <u>decided</u> that wearing pink made her look too pale.

DEEP POV: Glancing into the bathroom mirror, Amy grimaced. Pink was so *not* her color.

SHALLOW: I wanted to go to the movies with Jack, but then <u>decided</u> I was too tired to go.

DEEP POV: I already said I'd go the movies with Jack, but I couldn't stop yawning. Maybe he'd take a rain check.

SHALLOW: The second he touched me I <u>decided</u> I wasn't scared of him anymore.

DEEP POV: The instant he softly touched my arm, my fear dissolved.

SHALLOW: "Beneath all the dirt, he's not half bad looking," the woman <u>decided</u>.

DEEP POV: The woman eyed him closely. "You know, beneath all the dirt, he's not half bad looking."

***

Those examples should give you a clear idea how the word *decided* can weigh down your writing and distance your readers. Here is one more that should help. The first example lacks "voice" and it is weighed down with author intrusion and shallow writing.

SHALLOW:

Carmen <u>decided</u> to raise her hand up to the spot where she'd <u>felt</u> the offending prickle against her flesh and <u>touched</u> it, her fingers <u>feeling</u> chilled against the warmer spot on her skin. Something must have bitten her, she <u>decided</u>.

Great. Now I'll die of a spider bite, she <u>thought</u>. But even at her attempt to humor herself, she almost <u>felt</u> tears stinging her eyes.

DEEP POV:

Carmen lifted her hand to gently touch the wound where the offending prickle against her skin ached and rubbed it lightly. Her fingertips were ice cold against the warmer spot. Odd. Something must've bitten her.

"Great. Now I'll die of a spider bite," she mumbled.

But even with her attempt at humor, tears stung behind her eyes.

***

Hope these examples help you to revise your own stories into Deeper POV!

SHALLOW: WONDERED

If the reader is already inside a character's head, then the writer doesn't need to state that *he/she wondered / wonder / pondering / ponder* when we could proceed directly to whatever it was that the character is wondering about by using Deep POV.

Eliminate this filter word: WONDERED

SHALLOW: I wonder if it will rain this afternoon, he pondered.

DEEP POV: Uh-oh. Those clouds were coming in fast. He put on his raincoat just in case.

SHALLOW: I pondered life's meaning after losing my husband.

DEEP POV: Sitting alone in my room with our wedding album sitting on my lap, I sobbed openly. *How could I go on without him?*

SHALLOW: She pondered last night's strange events.

DEEP POV: Too many freaky things happened last night for her to ignore.

SHALLOW: Cassie <u>wondered</u> if Drake was single.

DEEP POV: Cassie flirtatiously winked at Drake. *Hmmm, no ring on his left hand.* Must be her lucky day!

SHALLOW: She <u>wondered</u> if they'd serve chocolate cake at the wedding.

DEEP POV: She walked over to the towering wedding cake. Yum. Hopefully, it was chocolate—her favorite!

SHALLOW: I eyed Marcus and <u>wondered</u> if he had finished his essay on time.

DEEP POV: I sighed heavily. Marcus was going to flunk if he didn't finish that essay on time.

SHALLOW: Sam gazed at the new car in the showroom and <u>wondered</u> if he could afford it.

DEEP POV: The brand new car sparkled in the morning light. If Sam cut back on his other expenses, he could afford to drive that baby out of the showroom within two months.

SHALLOW: I <u>wondered</u> where Stacy was.

DEEP POV: Where the heck was Stacy? Third time she'd been late for work this week.

SHALLOW: Kami <u>wondered</u> why she was always picked last at P.E.

DEEP POV: When the second to last kid was chosen for the soccer team, Kami inwardly groaned. It sucked always being picked last.

SHALLOW: I <u>wondered</u> for a second if he was going to stab Paul with his fork.

DEEP POV: For a second, it seemed like he was going to skewer smart aleck Paul with his fork.

SHALLOW: Lynn <u>wondered</u> frantically which element would be the best to summon if she needed to fight.

DEEP POV: Lynn scratched her chin. Which element would be the best to summon if I need to fight?

***

The following two examples demonstrate first what your sentences might look like with that annoying, visible narrator "telling" the story, and then what they might look like with the narrator eliminated.

SHALLOW:

Jennifer <u>wondered</u> if there would ever be a time when she could stop being careful. If there would ever be a time when she could use all of her powers. She <u>missed</u> it. It <u>felt</u> like part of her had been numbed.

She <u>pondered</u> if Susie and Michael cared about losing them. They acted as if it didn't bother them, but Jennifer <u>wondered</u> if it did. Living without using her powers was like having a pair of huge wings—but not being able to fly.

There's no point in <u>thinking</u> about it, <u>she told herself</u>. But Jennifer <u>wondered</u> if she used her powers openly, if it might be dangerous like the warlocks warned.

DEEP POV:

Jennifer drummed her manicured fingernails on the table.

When could she stop being so careful? Use her other powers?

Her heart lurched. Without using her magical powers, her body felt numb like it had been injected with Novocain. Almost dead.

Maybe Susie and Michael didn't care about things like that. But Jennifer sure did. It sucked not being able to use her powers anymore. It was like having big, beautiful wings—but never being able to soar above the clouds.

Jennifer sighed and hung her head. No need to keep stressing it. The warlocks repeatedly warned about using their powers in public. They could all end up dead. Period.

***

In upcoming chapters, I will explain and show you even more ways to remove shallow writing, in addition to offering the techniques necessary to perform these revisions.

SHALLOW: NOTICED

Another shallow type of "telling" that I frequently see in the manuscripts that I critique is the overuse of the word *notice / noticed.* It is considered a very shallow word, and one that can be easily removed to stay in Deeper POV.

By revising the filter word(s), the story becomes much more immediate and intriguing. The outcome is worth the extra effort to remain in Deep POV.

If you find a shallow word like "noticed" then also look for variants such as: *noticing, notice, realize, realized, realizing,* etc. You get the idea.

Eliminate this filter word: NOTICE

SHALLOW: I <u>noticed</u> for the first time that her hair was no longer crimson. Instead, her blond locks were streaked with dark purple.

DEEP POV: Her crimson highlights were now dyed a deep purple hue.

SHALLOW: I <u>noticed</u> Diego making his way toward the lobby.

DEEP POV: Diego marched toward the lobby.

SHALLOW: I <u>noticed</u> that there was something tucked inside the book.

DEEP POV: A piece of paper stuck out of the book, and I opened it to read the note.

SHALLOW: I was about to take my usual seat when I <u>noticed</u> that the schedule on the desk wasn't mine.

DEEP POV: Just as I was about to plop down on my seat, I squinted. That schedule on the desk wasn't mine.

SHALLOW: He <u>noticed</u> that the wrinkle between her eyebrows appeared whenever she was worried.

DEEP POV: That slight wrinkle formed between her eyebrows. She must be worried about something.

SHALLOW: She found herself looking at his mouth, and <u>noticed</u> that scar on his chin.

DEEP POV: She stared at his mouth, before her gaze lowered to a scar on his chin.

SHALLOW: Emily <u>noticed</u> Travis stayed right beside her.

DEEP POV: Travis stayed close to Emily's side.

SHALLOW: Hazel <u>noticed</u> my expression and smiled.

DEEP POV: Hazel glanced over and smiled at my expression.

SHALLOW: Halley <u>noticed</u> Isabel smirking at the mascot.

DEEP POV: Halley titled her head and caught Isabel smirking at the mascot.

***

Revising shallow writing should be one of the last things a writer does on their final draft, but once you become more aware of these "telling" words, then the easier it will become to avoid them in the first place. There are times when leaving the word *notice* in a sentence is needed, but most of the time it can be removed and the sentence rewritten into Deeper POV.

This next longer example should give you a stronger understanding of *show vs. tell.*

SHALLOW:

"Hi. I'm Anna Woodburn," my cousin said, and I <u>noticed</u> her long brown hair tumbled over her one shoulder.

"David Allen," the guy replied.

I <u>noticed</u> that David was wearing a dark wool coat although it was summer.

"And that's my friend, Kristen," David said, lifting his hand toward the pretty girl, who I <u>noticed</u> wore a thin white dress with a long, delicate gold necklace.

"Hey," she said.

"I'm Beth," I said, and looked downward, <u>noticing</u> that I needed a pedicure.

Looking up, I <u>noticed</u> that Kristen's gaze trailed over me as if analyzing my outfit. I <u>noticed</u> a swanky confidence about her, which wasn't all that surprising considering how lovely she was.

"I like your haircut," she mused, touching a red curl.

"Thanks." I <u>felt</u> myself squirm under her touch.

DEEP POV:

"Hi. I'm Anna Woodburn," my cousin said, her long brown hair tumbling over her one bare shoulder.

"David Allen," the guy replied.

I lifted an eyebrow. David was wearing a dark wool coat although it was a hot summer day. Really, really weird.

"And that's my friend, Kristen." David lifted his hand toward the pretty girl, who wore a white dress with a long, delicate gold necklace.

"Hey," she said.

"I'm, um, Beth," I mumbled, and looked downward at my sandals. The polish on my toes was chipped and the skin dry. *Yuk!* I was in serious need of a pedicure.

Looking up, I caught Kristen's gaze trailing over me as if she were a fashion designer analyzing her work. She had a classy confidence about her, which wasn't surprising considering how lovely she was.

"I adore your haircut," she mused, touching a red curl.

I squirmed under her touch. "Oh, thanks."

***

Deeper POV allows a reader to actively participate in the scene and ignites the reader's imagination, as well as helps them to forget that they're *just* reading a story. And a reader who feels like they're vividly experiencing the narrative is a reader who won't be able to put your story down.

SHALLOW: WISHED

As you revise your scenes, remember that Deep POV will help to lure the reader into each character's head so completely that your readers will feel as if they are experiencing everything that happens right alongside your narrator.

The commonly overused filter words *wish / wished / hope / hoped* can make your writing become shallow.

Eliminate this filter word: WISHED

SHALLOW: I wished that I could confide in him.

DEEP POV: Staring at Drake, I chewed on a strand of my hair. No way could I tell him the truth.

SHALLOW: Cam wishes he had bought that newer TV.

DEEP POV: Watching the football game on Carl's new flat-screen only drove home the fact that Cam should've bought one for himself.

SHALLOW: He <u>wished</u> he could help.

DEEP POV: He yearned to help the others, but he was forbidden.

SHALLOW: Claire <u>wished</u> things could have been different.

DEEP POV: If only things could've been different.

SHALLOW: She <u>wished</u> that she had a fairy godmother to tell her what to do.

DEEP POV: What she needed was a fairy godmother to tell her what to do.

SHALLOW: Cindy <u>wished</u> that she could go back in time.

DEEP POV: Going back in time would be the only way to fix this mess.

Eliminate this filter word: HOPED

SHALLOW: She <u>hoped</u> Ryan would forgive her before the weekend.

DEEP POV: Ryan just had to forgive her before the weekend started.

SHALLOW: I just <u>hoped</u> I wasn't deluding myself with optimism.

DEEP POV: Now was not the time to delude myself with optimism.

SHALLOW: She <u>hoped</u> he couldn't hear the tightness in her throat.

DEEP POV: Maybe he hadn't sensed the tightness in her throat.

SHALLOW: Grabbing the ax, I hoped it would slow down any zombies who decided to pursue us.

DEEP POV: I grabbed the ax. Now this baby would slow down any zombies who were stupid enough to pursue us.

SHALLOW: She <u>hoped</u> he would get home first.

DEEP POV: If she slowed her steps, he might get home first.

***

This next example is longer and filled with those dreaded "telling" words that make the writing shallow and create narrative distance.

SHALLOW:

Dallas <u>watched</u> her emerge from the kitchen and <u>saw</u> her crossing in front of the windows, a bottle of beer in one hand. He <u>thought</u> it was something dark and bitter. Dallas <u>knew</u> she didn't like light beer. He <u>wished</u> now that he'd brought a six-pack with him on the stakeout.

His shoulders <u>felt</u> tight and he shrugged. He <u>felt</u> sweat wetting his shirt as he <u>watched</u> her switch on her stereo. She tipped her head back, closed her eyes, and her body moved to the music. Dallas <u>wished</u> he <u>knew</u> what she was listening to. He had no clue.

I bet it's a soft classical piece, he <u>thought</u>.

DEEP POV:

She emerged from the kitchen, crossing in front of the windows with a beer in one hand. Something dark and bitter. She didn't go for cheap light beer.

Dallas shrugged his tense shoulders, sweat dampening the back of his shirt. Stakeouts were brutal. He shifted in the driver's seat, trying to get more comfortable.

Through the binoculars, his gaze tracked her every moment as she switched on the stereo. Her head lolled backward, her eyes closing, her body seductively swaying to the tempo.

What was she listening to? Jazz, rock, country, or some popular pop song?

He had no idea. Dallas bet it was a smooth classical piece. Light, timeless, elegant.

***

Just to be clear again, "telling" or *naming the emotion* isn't always the wrong way to write a sentence or convey an emotion. It doesn't always lead to weaker, shallow writing. *Showing vs. telling* is all about finding a good balance.

SHALLOW: REALIZED

The primary goal of fiction is to entertain and offer escapism. For a few hours each day while we're reading a good book, we get to be someone else, visit exotic lands, and experience new things. So, to really experience these things, a writer should apply the Deep POV technique.

Even if we think that we understand the difference between *showing* vs *telling*, shallow writing can sneak into our stories. A few red flags that you can easily search for in your current WIP (work-in-progress) is use of the word *realize / realized / realization*, which can take you out of Deep POV.

Eliminate this filter word: REALIZED

SHALLOW: I should have <u>realized</u> that right then was a good time to run.

DEEP POV: This might be a good time to run!

SHALLOW: I suddenly <u>realized</u> I didn't want to be left alone.

DEEP POV: The house was too lonely and quiet, and I had the sudden urge to escape.

SHALLOW: I realized that I'd totally spaced out on what she'd been saying.

DEEP POV: I blinked out of my daze and said, "Um, do you mind repeating that?"

SHALLOW: Alone in her room, she realized that on some level, Mark was right.

DEEP POV: Alone in her room, she sat down on the bed and sighed. Mark had been right about everything.

SHALLOW: They were at the beach, he realized.

DEEP POV: Damn, they must be at the beach already.

SHALLOW: Chandra finally realized the gravity of her faux pas.

DEEP POV: Chandra groaned at her obvious social blunder.

SHALLOW: He isn't coming home, she realized.

DEEP POV: As the sun rose in the east, she sighed. He wasn't coming home.

SHALLOW: Then with a start of fear, realization hit him. It had been his sister stealing the car parts.

DEEP POV: Clutching at collar of his shirt, he groaned. If the mobsters found out it that it was his sister stealing the car parts, they were both doomed.

SHALLOW: I had a <u>startling realization</u> (Cliché) that he wasn't human.

DEEP POV: Stumbling backward, I leaned on the wall. He wasn't human!

SHALLOW: A dizzy feeling swept over me with the <u>realization</u> that I could cast spells.

DEEP POV: Dizziness assaulted me. I could actually cast spells!

These next two examples are a bit longer and they will give you a clear-cut idea on how to revise shallow writing into riveting prose.

As you revise, keep in mind that especially in first-person POV, there are much better ways for the protagonist to convey to the reader that they're aware of their actions than simply stating it by using words like *realize / realized*.

This next excerpt was taken from my novel SHATTERED SILENCE (book two) and has a "before" revisions and an "after" reversions example.

SHALLOW:

At the Jeep, I fell forward, and <u>felt</u> myself panting and <u>saw</u> dirt rising around me, as I looked back at the clearing.

My breath was ragged and my chest felt like it was ready to explode. For only a moment, I rested against the bumper. Relief gradually hit me when I realized that the howling sounds in the woods hadn't followed me.

What a big coward I was turning out to be, I realized. I knew Evans would be ashamed.

Opening the door to the Jeep, I sat on the seat and locked myself inside. I felt my hands shaking and I realized that it took me five tries to get the engine started. The Jeep made a loud sound, and I felt a breath push itself past my lips.

"Just get home."

I realized that I had said the words repeatedly as I drove home. I wouldn't think about what had just happened.

I was only sixteen, I thought, but at that moment, I suddenly wished I had my dad right then. He gave good hugs.

I knew this was bad. Real bad.

And I knew that I was fooling myself if I thought I was ready to take on paranormals. And I realized that my magick had been infected by Esael's blood.

I realized that Evans was right about my demon brand.

DEEP POV:

At the Jeep, I fell forward onto my knees, panting for breath—dirt rising around me—and stared back at the clearing.

My breath was ragged and my chest heaved like it was ready to explode. For only a moment, I rested against the bumper. My body somewhat relaxed. Thankfully, the howling *thing* in the woods hadn't followed me.

What a big coward I was turning out to be. Some demon hunter. Evans would be so ashamed.

Opening the creaky door to the Jeep, I hopped onto the seat and locked myself inside. My hands were shaking so hard that it took me five tries to get the engine started. The Jeep rumbled to life, and a breath pushed itself past my lips.

"Just get home." I said the words repeatedly as I drove. I wouldn't think about what had just happened. Couldn't think about what had just happened.

Ah, hell! I was only sixteen, but at that moment I suddenly wanted nothing as much as I wanted my dad right then. He gave the best hugs in the world. Hugs that made everything awful seem so much better. Not so terrible.

Because this was bad. Real bad.

And I was fooling myself if I thought I was ready to take on paranormals. Or that my white magick hadn't been infected by Esael's evil blood.

Evans was right about one thing. I had been branded by a freakin' demon.

***

In a first draft, the words can flow out of us in creative mode, but when it's time to edit and streamline our prose, writers should step back with deliberate wisdom and skill and rewrite shallow scenes into Deeper POV whenever we can.

DESCRIBE THE SENSES

To write using the Deep POV technique, writers should involve all of the five senses in their emotional descriptions. Try to vividly describe every sensation, reaction, and emotion that your character(s) is experiencing.

Remember that "telling" a reader what a character is feeling or experiencing is *not* using Deep POV. The right way is to show by describing what is unfolding in every scene by the use of action, description, dialogue, and the five senses.

Powerful descriptive writing should always strive to involve the use of every human sense. It is also a great way of making your scenes three-dimensional. In order to do this, I think it's important to stay in Deep POV to construct a more realistic and engaging scene. Because if we don't, as writers, we are cheating our readers by limiting their use of the five senses in our scenes, or by not using them at all.

SHALLOW (touch): I <u>touched</u> the dress to <u>feel</u> the fabric.

DEEP POV: My fingers caressed the silky fabric.

If you're going to describe how something tastes, sounds and looks, then you can leave out how it feels and smells. You never want to assault your reader's senses, or they will skip ahead to get back to the action.

There are many ways to achieve Deep POV, but here are a few sure-fire ways to enhance your prose.

THE MAIN FIVE SENSES ARE:

- **Sight**: What your character sees. Describe images and the setting through their eyes.

- **Hear:** Noises that surround your character(s) in every scene.

- **Smell**: Make clear the scents, aromas, and odors.

- **Touch**: Show the feel of icy snow or the luxurious feel of silk sheets.

- **Taste**: Describe the tart flavor of a lime or the harsh burn and acrid taste of whiskey.

***

Below I have provided some examples of the wrong way to describe something and the correct way through use of Deep POV by including the five senses. The filter words are underlined.

SHALLOW (touch): I <u>felt</u> cold when I stepped outside the warm house.

DEEP POV: The chilly winds nipped at my cheeks and I shuddered.

SHALLOW (scent): Lori could <u>smell</u> the trees and pine scents in the air.

DEEP POV: Aromas drifted from the meadow—pine and cedar—as a strong gust blew across the rippling lake.

SHALLOW (sight): I <u>could see</u> Malcolm walking toward me.

DEEP POV: Malcolm strode toward me with a brisk gait.

SHALLOW (hear): I <u>heard</u> ghostly moans coming from within the haunted house.

DEEP POV: Ghostly moans came from within the haunted house.

SHALLOW (taste): The steak was burnt and <u>tasted</u> nasty.

DEEP POV: He bit into the blackened piece of meat, the steak had a charred flavor.

***

As writers, we want our readers to experience the story through the senses of our characters. And by engaging the five senses, plus describing the emotional reactions, it helps readers engage more closely with the character's experience. Shallow writing can and *will* have the opposite effect.

Please compare the next two examples.

SHALLOW:

When Scott <u>heard</u> the growling <u>sound</u>, he <u>looked</u> down and <u>saw</u> a large dog blocking the trail. He <u>knew</u> it would attack if he moved. Scott <u>felt</u> a sense of <u>terror</u> build in his heart.

DEEP POV:

Scott halted at the warning growl. Standing in front of him was a large dog, flashing its teeth. He stifled the girlish shriek that leaked from his lips with one hand. His heart jackhammered in his chest as he took a stumbling step backward.

***

Can you tell the difference?

In the second example, you can imagine much more vividly the dog and Scott's emotional response. It is always better to attempt to make your scene unique by inserting some of the five senses into the narrative.

Now try to use these examples as inspiration to revise your WIP by using some of the five senses in your own writing.

DESCRIBE THE EMOTIONS

This chapter will include even more great ways to "show" emotion through vivid description without *stating it* to the reader. Try to describe what the character is feeling or experiencing. All well-written novels share one thing in common—character emotion.

The best way to convey your character's thoughts, senses, emotions, and feelings is to *show* them though powerful description. To do this, try depicting the character's physical reactions along with the emotional ones.

Remember to always use the concept of the *show and don't tell* in your fiction writing. This tenet means describing what a character is feeling without actually "telling" the reader what the feeling is. Showing takes a lot more creativity than "telling," but trust me, it will pay off by giving your readers a much more powerful and believable story.

Eliminate filter words and show emotions instead.

SHALLOW: "Go get it," he said <u>angrily</u>, slamming his fist on the table.

DEEP POV: He slapped his meaty fist on the table with a force that rattled the glasses. When he spoke, his voice held an ominous quality. "Get it *now*."

***

Strive to *show* immediate reactions through active physical gestures, emotional responses, clever dialogue, and action descriptors. There aren't any hard or fast rules, but often a character's reaction to something usually follows this order:

- *physical (involuntary) reaction*

- *emotional response*

- *thought / deliberation*

- *dialogue (internal or external)*

- *purposeful action / decision*

If you write a character's reactions in this simple order, it will usually give a stronger visual image in your reader's mind, and the reader will experience the emotions along with your character.

It seems to me that even bestselling authors overuse the biggest offender of "telling," which is the word: *felt*. Most of the time using this word causes narrative distance.

In most cases, emotional description shouldn't be too specific. The reader should know without being told with shallow writing that the character is, for instance, frightened. It is always better to use stronger words like *shudder, startle, froze,* or *turned away* to show emotions and not use nonspecific "telling words" like *surprise, afraid, joy, terror*, or *disappointment*.

I have included an example of intense emotions, effective dialogue tags, and realistic reactions that are written in Deep POV.

This excerpt was taken from my novel MOONLIGHT MAYHEM (book three in my Spellbound series). The heroine, Shiloh, has recently broken up with her boyfriend and this is the first time they've seen each other in weeks. Notice how her inner monologue flows naturally with the external conversation and action—all written in Deeper POV.

DEEP POV:

Then the swoon-worthy Trent Donovan sauntered into the restaurant. My ex with the smoldering eyes—*yeah, I'm a total girl*—and the wide shoulders. Trent with the charming, intimate habit of sweeping the hair from my face. Trent with the electrifying touch…

Dammit. I had to stop going all fangirl every time I saw him!

Still, the air whooshed from my lungs. I closed my eyes and took a deep breath. When I opened them, I swear my body froze. My heart stopped beating. A volatile, insistent thrill shot through my veins, and I shuddered.

Ariana jerked her chin at the counter. "Uh-oh. Ex-boyfriend at one o'clock."

Lifting my head, I groaned. "Maybe he won't spot us."

"Unless you know an invisibility spell, Trent's got natural radar when it comes to you."

My hands trembled in my lap. My stomach pitched and rolled. I had no place to hide. I was tempted to get up and run out the door before he noticed me…

***

Could you see, feel, and sense the character's emotions? Good.

Now open up your manuscript and start revising your own stories into Deep POV to create a gripping narrative that your readers will be unable to put down.

In the succeeding chapters, I have listed tons of helpful examples of filter words that take you out of Deep POV. Again, all of these examples have already been used in my published books, but they should help spark your own creative muse and give you some ideas on how to modify your own wonderful stories.

By giving your characters *real* emotions and reactions, it gives them even more realism. Being able to describe those emotions through Deep POV adds mastery to your writing. Add your character's five senses to describe how he/she is feeling without *naming the emotion*, and watch your scenes come vividly to life.

EMOTION: EXCITEMENT

In the next several chapters, I will offer some great examples on how to rewrite the most commonly used emotional descriptors. Since this handbook would be thousands of pages long if I listed them all, I have narrowed down the biggest offenders to the most frequently used "telling'" emotional descriptors that can make your writing become shallow.

Within most of the early drafts that I edit for my clients, I notice an abundance of shallow words like: *excited, excitement, exhilaration, exhilarated, anticipation, anticipate, and anticipated,* which can take you out of Deep POV.

However, like I stated before, sometimes *naming the emotion* is perfectly acceptable, but only if it helps create easier readability.

Still not convinced?

By applying the Deep POV method, your writing will become more alive and intriguing. Try it and you'll notice an immediate difference. Your readers will be able to actively relate to whatever your characters are feeling or experiencing in that moment.

(For a more comprehensive list of emotional traits, please check out the reference book: "*The Emotion Thesaurus: A Writer's Guide to Character Expression*")

Some physical signs of excitement might be:

Body vibrating with anticipation

Hands trembling

Heart swelling

Jumping up and down

Laughing out loud

Hugging people

Bouncing on balls of feet

Rocking on heels

Unable to sit still

Talking quickly

Squealing and raising voice or screaming

Pumping fist into the air

Skin buzzing

Huge smile

Dancing around

Heart racing

Lightheaded

Rapidly waving hands in the air (Jazz hands)

Shaking head with grin

Clutching at heart

Examples of the emotion: EXCITED

SHALLOW: I felt <u>excited</u> and alive for the first time in months.

DEEP POV: For the first time in months, I smiled at everyone I passed on the street.

SHALLOW: "This is gonna be awesome!" he said, his voice thrumming with <u>excitement</u>.

DEEP POV: He was practically jumping up and down as if he had ants in his pants. "This is gonna be awesome!" he exclaimed.

SHALLOW: My heart started pounding with <u>excitement</u>.

DEEP POV: My heartbeat sped up and I bounced on my toes.

SHALLOW: <u>Excitement</u> sang through her, and it was all she could do to stand still.

DEEP POV: Her body thrummed with energy as she rocked on her heels.

SHALLOW: A tremor of <u>excitement</u> crept up his spine.

DEEP POV: He shivered and let out a throaty laugh.

SHALLOW: "So Isaac's going to sit with us tomorrow, too?" she asked <u>excitedly</u>.

DEEP POV: Bouncing in her seat, she asked, "So Isaac's going to sit with us tomorrow, too?"

SHALLOW: Catarina's heart fluttered in <u>excitement</u>. (Cliché)

DEEP POV: Catarina's heart fluttered and her big blue eyes sparkled.

SHALLOW: I <u>felt</u> a rush of <u>excitement</u>. (Cliché)

DEEP POV: A tingle spread throughout my body and warmed my heart.

SHALLOW: His lopsided smile <u>sent</u> a sweet burst of <u>excitement</u> through her.

DEEP POV: At the sight of his lopsided smile, her skin prickled and a pleasant buzz flowed through her.

SHALLOW: She gasped, <u>sending</u> a tremor of <u>excitement</u> up his spine.

DEEP POV: When she gasped, a quivery tremor shot up his spine.

SHALLOW: "I don't believe it," he says with <u>a spark of amusement in his eyes</u>. (Cliché)

DEEP POV: "I don't believe it," he says, his eyes crinkling up into a smile.

***

The following examples from my own novel RECKLESS RE-VENGE (book four) illustrates how to revise shallow scenes into Deeper POV by eliminating the weaker "telling" words from the sentences.

SHALLOW:

"Tonight sad thoughts are not allowed," Trent said <u>enthusiastically</u>. "At least for three hours."

"How exactly do you intend to do that?" I asked <u>eagerly</u>.

"Maybe like..." He said and leaned over the console to kiss my mouth.

A warm rush of <u>excitement</u> hit me. I smiled at my boyfriend. "Good start."

"Just you wait." He shifted back and chuckled deep in his throat. That's the way a laugh should be, I <u>thought</u>.

Soft music seeped through the speakers and I <u>realized</u> that I was humming along.

"If you like this playlist, I can burn you a mix CD to load it into your iPod," Trent said.

"Sure," I said excitedly.

Trent wore a happy smile as he took my hand and I felt a jolt. His hand was warm and rough. I knew that my smile had widened. I felt my heart pounding so hard I couldn't do anything else.

As excitement bubbled up inside me, I wondered if tonight was going to be fun.

DEEP POV:

"Well, tonight deep thoughts are not allowed. Only fun," he said. "I consider it my duty to make you forget all about your troubles. At least for a few hours."

"Oh? And how exactly do you intend to do that?"

"Like this." He leaned over the console and kissed me hard on the mouth.

A rush of warmth hit my skin. I smiled at my hotheaded, crazy, yet loveable boyfriend. "That's a good start."

"There's more where that came from, sweetheart." He shifted back into his seat and chuckled, a throaty, uninhibited laugh. The way a laugh should be.

The almost hypnotic sounds of *Lifehouse*'s "You and Me" seeped through the speakers and I hummed along with the tune.

"If you like this playlist, I can burn you a mix CD to load onto your iPod," Trent offered.

My grin widened. "Yes, please!"

Trent's face broke into that killer smile as he took my hand and a jolt shot through me. His hand was warm and vaguely rough, his grip confident and steady. My heart was pounding so hard I couldn't do anything else. Tonight was sure to be loads of fun.

***

Did you compare the last two examples? Are you starting to grasp how shallow writing pulls the reader out of the story? Good!

Naming the emotion is a bad habit that writers easily fall into, which focuses the storyline on "telling" rather than "showing."

EMOTION: FRUSTRATION

There is usually no need to *name the emotion*. A reader will understand the emotional reactions without the writer stuffing their prose with extra information like a slap to the face. Don't be afraid to be subtle in your storytelling. Trust me, readers will be grateful that you are respecting their intelligence.

These offending "telling" words like *frustrated, frustration, aggravated, irritated, annoyed, exasperated,* can be found in almost every published novel that you read, but should be revised whenever possible for Deeper POV.

Some physical signs of frustration might be:

Brain feels tied up in knots

Talking to inanimate objects

Constant pacing

Urge to throw something

Bunch hands into fists

Snap a pencil

Punch whatever is in front of character: wall, pillow, locker, tree, etc.

Slapping the antagonist

Heart beating more quickly

Breath speeds up

Body shaking

Tapping a pencil or pen

Jiggling keys

Biting lip

Drumming fingers on table or desk

Examples of the emotion: FRUSTRATED

SHALLOW: A bout of frustration churns inside me.

DEEP POV: Pinching my lips together, I stomp my foot.

SHALLOW: The vampire slayer rushed at me with a scream of frustration and buried the stake in my chest.

DEEP POV: The vampire slayer rushed forward with jerky movements and plunged the wooden stake into my heart.

SHALLOW: "No! It's not like that," I said, suddenly <u>frustrated</u>.

DEEP POV: Clenching my jaw, I blurted, "*No!* It's not like that."

SHALLOW: <u>Frustration</u> flicked across Jerrod's face. (Cliché)

DEEP POV: Jarrod snorted and threw his hands up in the air.

SHALLOW: Nikki groaned in <u>frustration</u>. (Cliché)

DEEP POV: Groaning, Nikki dropped her head in her hands.

SHALLOW: <u>Frustration</u> bubbled in my veins. "Accept it. Lisa has a new boyfriend."

DEEP POV: I just wanted to reach out and grab him. Slap him as hard as I could. Instead, I blurted, "Just accept it! Lisa has moved on, and so should *you*."

SHALLOW: She was <u>angry</u> and <u>frustrated</u>. (Cliché)

DEEP POV: Pulling at her hair, she grumbled, "Just stop it!"

SHALLOW: Jack <u>looked</u> <u>frustrated</u>.

DEEP POV: Jack jiggled the keys in his pocket, and a muscle ticked in his jaw.

SHALLOW: Edward made a <u>frustrated</u> noise in the back of his throat.

DEEP POV: Edward grunted low in his throat and shoved his hands under his arms.

***

These subsequent two examples exemplify how to modify shallow sentences into Deeper POV by eradicating the filter words from any scene.

SHALLOW:

At the start of class, I <u>noticed</u> Holly walk over to me with an <u>irritated</u> expression. "I don't know what the hell you think you're doing, harassing Elden like that," she <u>hissed</u>.

Although I was <u>startled</u> and <u>frustrated</u> by her badgering, I managed an <u>innocent</u> look. "I have no idea what you're talking about, Holly."

She frowned at me in <u>anger</u> for a moment, and then turned away with a toss of her messy hair. "I was just trying to save you some awkwardness, Luce," she said, in a <u>frustrated</u> voice. "He likes me now."

I <u>felt</u> my face turning red. Though I <u>knew</u> Holly was just being a jealous brat, I couldn't help <u>worrying</u> that she might be right.

Maybe Elden *was* just being nice to me because he felt sorry for me. I <u>felt</u> more and more <u>depressed</u> as the class dragged on.

I <u>wondered</u> when the bell would ring and I'd be able to escape.

DEEP POV:

As the warning bell rang, Holly entered the classroom and marched over to me with a nasty twinkle in her eye. "What the hell do you think you're doing? Stalking Elden?" she spat. "Do I need to remind you that he's my boyfriend now?"

My body tensed up and I flinched at her harsh tone. My eyes grew wide and I said in my sweetest voice, "I have no idea what you're babbling on about, Holly. You're not actually worried that Elden might still like me?"

She glared in silence, and I swear smoke was pouring out of her ears. Finally, she turned away with a toss of her windblown hair and sauntered over to her own desk. But she wanted to have the last word. So typical.

"Just trying to keep you from making an ass out of yourself, Luce," she said, in a high-pitched voice. "He likes me now. Got it?"

My face turned red and I slumped in my seat. Holly was just being her usual hateful self. But what if she was right?

Maybe Elden *was* just being nice because he felt sorry for me. I shouldn't let Holly get under my skin, but my shoulders sagged and I hung my head.

The clock ticked slowly and class dragged.

When was the damn bell gonna ring so I could escape?

***

Do a search to find the filter words in your own story if you want to revise into Deeper POV. There are times when *naming the emotion* will add to the rhythm of your sentence and it is simply necessary, but when you're writing in Deeper POV, you should try to avoid doing so.

EMOTION: DISAPPOINTMENT

Writers create narrative distance and author intrusion when they deliberately or unintentionally insert shallow POV and "telling" words into their scenes.

These examples for the shallow word *disappointed / disappointment* should offer creative ways to avoid identifying the emotion, which only serves to distance the reader.

Some physical signs of disappointment might be:

Mouth turning downward

Tears burning eyes

Tipping chin downward and frowning

Heavy sighing

Pain in chest

Swaying on feet

Sluggishness

Puckering brow

Leaning on wall

Dropping head into hands

Shaking head and crying

Stomach hurting

Crawling into bed and hiding

Locking yourself in a bathroom

Weeping in shower

Examples of the emotion: DISAPPOINTED

SHALLOW: He was <u>disappointed</u> that Rachel stood him up.

DEEP POV: Lowering his head, he shuffled into the movie alone. Rachel had stood him up for the last time.

SHALLOW: Bitter <u>disappointment</u> pricked Julianna's chest because she didn't get the lead in the school play.

DEEP POV: Shoulders drooping, Julianna blinked back tears. No way would she cry at school over not getting the lead role.

SHALLOW: Michele <u>felt</u> so <u>disappointed</u> that she'd failed her driving test again.

DEEP POV: Lips pressed tight, Michele dragged her feet all the way home. *Can't believe I failed that test. Again.*

SHALLOW: For the third year in a row, I was <u>disappointed</u> about not being picked for the swim team.

DEEP POV: Looking up with her hands raised skyward, she mumbled, "Why does this *always* happen to me?"

SHALLOW: A stab of <u>disappointment</u> punched Amanda in the gut.

DEEP POV: Covering her face with her hands, Amanda sighed loudly. "This majorly sucks," she muttered.

SHALLOW: How many more <u>disappointments</u> would Alex have to endure until he found another job?

DEEP POV: Tilting his chin downward and frowning, Alex sat down heavily on the bed. He was so sick of being a jobless loser.

SHALLOW: My voice was low, severe and acrid <u>disappointment</u> tied knots in my gut.

DEEP POV: My voice sounded low, harsh—sour emotion tying knots in my gut.

SHALLOW: <u>Disappointment</u> swelled so quickly in my chest it trampled the passionate desire.

DEEP POV: Not meeting his eyes, the heat intensified in my chest and squelched the passionate desire.

SHALLOW: A spasm of <u>disappointment</u> hit me hard in the gut.

DEEP POV: My skin flushed. The whole thing was about a hundred levels of awkward and a warehouse full of someone -please-kill-me-now.

***

Here is another example of how to avoid *naming the emotion,* and instead show the character's reaction through the Deep POV technique.

SHALLOW:

I <u>looked around</u> me, at how empty the dining room was and <u>felt</u> a stab of <u>disappointment</u>. I <u>realized</u> that Andrea and the rest of my friends hadn't shown up yet to the party.

I <u>knew</u> I had texted everyone the night before with a reminder, but apparently no one was on time.

DEEP POV:

My heart squeezed. *This royally sucks.* Where is everyone?

I took in the empty dining room and breathed out through my mouth. Andrea and the rest of my friends should've been here by now. I'd texted everyone the night before with a reminder.

But damn if I was going to let their lateness ruin my birthday.

***

I hope these examples help you to rewrite scenes in your own manuscript or short story.

EMOTION: ANGER

Try to keep in mind that ALL actions should have a visceral, emotional, or physical reaction. Readers need to see a character's emotional and physical responses to almost *every* event that happens to them in your storyline. If he/she has no reaction to pinch or plot points, or inciting incidents, or overall story problems, then it's as if those actions and revelations have no meaning. If they mean nothing to the character, then they mean nothing to the plot or to the reader.

To stay in Deep POV, it's redundant to be told that the character is "angry." It is so much more interesting to *show* how the character reacts. In order to show these emotional reactions, try to omit "telling" words such as: *anger, angry, fury, furious, rage, enraged, antagonism, wrath, annoyance, irritation, irritated, etc.* from your narrative.

Some physical signs of anger might be:

Face reddens or turns purple

Tension in body

Shouting or raising voice

Swearing

Crying

Punching something

Stomping or marching

Eyes flashing

Mouth quivering

Slamming door

Ears get hot / red

Flaring nostrils

Examples of the emotion: ANGER

SHALLOW: He looks very <u>angry</u>.

DEEP POV: His mouth is set in a grim line, jaw tense.

SHALLOW: <u>Anger</u> was simmering through my veins.

DEEP POV: Heat licked my skin, and my limbs vibrated. *He was dead meat!*

SHALLOW: My <u>anger</u> returns in full force.

DEEP POV: My fingers clutch tightly at the armrests, my nails digging into the soft fabric.

SHALLOW: A sudden rush of anger surfaces.

DEEP POV: My eyes narrow and my hands shake as I take a menacing step closer to my enemy.

SHALLOW: A red cloud of rage swam across Michael's vision.

DEEP POV: Michael's vision clouded with swarms of dark red.

SHALLOW: I tried to quell my jealousy and rage.

DEEP POV: My body twitched as I stared holes into my friend's back while she flirted away with the boy I was crushing on.

SHALLOW: When he spun back around, his face was drawn with fury.

DEEP POV: When he whirled back around, his eyes bulged and his jaw clenched.

SHALLOW: His face erupted into a map of surprise and rage.

DEEP POV: A vein in his forehead throbbed and he shook a fist in the air.

SHALLOW: She felt an absolute rage boiling inside her.

DEEP POV: An infusion of adrenaline rocked her body.

SHALLOW: Her face screwed-up into a twisted mass of rage.

DEEP POV: With her eyes flashing, her mouth twisted into an ugly sneer.

***

Here is a longer paragraph that indicates how you can revise the emotion *anger* into Deeper POV and engage your readers.

This excerpt is taken from my novel LOST IN STARLIGHT, and shows both the before revision and the published draft. The heroine just discovered that the guy she's crushing on might be dating another girl.

The first example has too much "telling" and no "voice" and the narrative is weighed down with extra words; however, the published excerpt has riveting "voice" and it is written in Deep POV.

SHALLOW:

I am angry with Hayden. "Let's just say last night was a mistake," I blurt, thinking I had better not waver.

Hayden takes my hand, and I feel my heart skip a beat. I look at his face, and think that his eyes are so amazing, but a burst of fresh anger still simmers in my gut.

"Please believe me, Sloane. It's over with Tama," he says. "And I *don't* want to pretend that last night never happened."

I pull my hand away and fury heats my chest. "Or maybe she's more your kind?"

Hayden appears uneasy. "Yes." He glances anxiously at my face. "Sloane, let me prove to you that I'm not a jerk. Have breakfast with me on the beach."

I do not want to be alone with him. I <u>know</u> I cannot trust myself.

I stare at him, and that <u>rage</u> resurfaces. He's such a liar, I <u>think</u>.

While he stays quiet, I try to <u>think</u> of a good excuse. Our relationship needs to be platonic. Because if I go with him, the whole time I'll just be <u>thinking</u> about kissing him.

"Well, Peaches?" he asks. "Can we talk?"

I have no plans today, and I can't even <u>think</u> up good lie. I <u>feel</u> very curious about Tama. But it might be a bad idea.

I <u>know</u> I shouldn't go with him or trust him, yet I <u>feel</u> my <u>rage</u> slipping away. I can't resist Hayden. I look into his eyes and all of the <u>anger</u> dissolves. I <u>know</u> that I will regret doing this.

"Fine." I say, <u>dejectedly</u>. "I'll go."

DEEP POV:

"Let's just say last night was a colossal mistake," I say firmly, resolved to stick to my guns.

Hayden takes my hand, causing my heart to skip an alarming number of beats. I hazard a glance at his face. Bad move. God, those remarkable eyes. A person could die happy just gazing into them. But. Not. Me. I will not be a weak, simpering ball of need.

"Please believe me, Sloane. It's over with Tama," he says in a soft voice. "And I *don't* want to pretend that last night never happened. We had a moment, right? You must've felt it, too."

"Was that the moment you had with me or with Tama?" I jerk my hand from his. "Or maybe she's more your kind? Is she a hybrid, too?"

Hayden kicks at the ground. "Yes." He glances anxiously at my face. "Just have breakfast with me, Sloane, so I can prove to you that I'm not a jerk."

Alone? With Hayden?

Don't do it. Do not do it.

I stare at him, imagining a giant neon sign above his head that reads: *WARNING! Lying-girlfriend-haver!*

While he stays quiet, I try to come up with a quick excuse. I cannot go. I need to keep this relationship strictly platonic. Because the whole time I'll just be thinking about kissing that perfect mouth. His soft, warm lips—

"Well, Peaches?" he asks. "Can we go someplace and talk?"

I shouldn't go, but I can't resist that strange, irresistible *pull* of Hayden. Another look in those incredible eyes and I'm a goner. I am *so* gonna regret this.

"Fine." A sigh creeps past my lips. "I'll go."

***

Did you see how Deep POV brings the scene and emotions effortlessly alive for the reader? Awesome!

We're inside main character's head throughout the entire second passage and experiencing her anger and frustration, and even confusion, right along with her as the scene unfolds.

EMOTION: SADNESS

By using the Deep POV technique, your readers will experience an instant connection with what's happening, and feel as though there is nothing between them and the narrative.

As you revise in Deep POV, you don't want your character's thoughts, actions, or emotions to be *told* or *explained* to the reader. Trust me, readers want to experience the events unfolding inside the character's head as they take place.

So, try to omit "telling" words like *sad, sadness, unhappy, miserable, depressed, gloomy, sorrow, wretched, dejected, forlorn, depression, sorrowful, woeful, cheerless* from your scenes.

Some physical signs of sadness might be:

Loss of appetite

Crawl into bed and cry

Tiredness

Drooping eyelids

Glossy or glassed eyes

Lips pulled down at corners

Numbness throughout your body

Sluggish movements

Trembling lips

Clutching blanket, stuffed animal, or pillow

Blubbering loudly

Closing eyes and not speaking

Feel as if moving (and thinking) in slow motion

Eyes bloodshot

Dark shadows under eyes

Examples of the emotion: SADNESS / GRIEF

SHALLOW: A <u>sad</u> <u>feeling</u> makes my heart hurt.

DEEP POV: A tight fist constricts around my heart.

SHALLOW: He sounds so <u>sad</u>.

DEEP POV: My heart clenches at his dejected tone.

SHALLOW: I feel <u>sad</u> and lonely now that Craig's dead.

DEEP POV: Sobbing into Craig's old T-shirt, my heart aches fiercely. *I miss him so much.*

SHALLOW: Feeling <u>unhappy</u>, I start to cry.

DEEP POV: Tears sting my eyes and I sniffle, wiping at my runny nose with my sleeve.

SHALLOW: <u>Grief</u> and <u>misery</u> make me feel like crying.

DEEP POV: My arms hang at my sides, my body slack. I clutch at my chest and sob uncontrollably.

SHALLOW: The <u>grief</u> and <u>frustration</u> welling up inside me needs an outlet.

DEEP POV: A surge of pain wells up inside me. Needing an outlet, I grab the stuffed bear and punch it.

SHALLOW: <u>Sadness</u> and <u>loneliness</u> washed over him.

DEEP POV: The constant ache in his chest was made worse whenever he visited Amy's grave.

SHALLOW: I <u>noticed</u> his eyes held a <u>touch of sadness</u>. (Cliché)

DEEP POV: As he looked away, I glimpsed the tears welling in his eyes.

SHALLOW: "Just go away," I said, feeling <u>miserable</u>.

DEEP POV: My face went slack and my voice dull, "Just go away."

SHALLOW: Lauren <u>felt</u> a pang of <u>grief</u> as she went to work.

DEEP POV: Drooping her shoulders, Lauren shuffled into work.

SHALLOW: Jaime just looked at her feet, <u>miserable</u>.

DEEP POV: Jaime stared down at her feet with glossy eyes.

***

The following excerpt is from the third book in my Spellbound series, MOONLIGHT MAYHEM, where the heroine has just lost her father and she is overcome with grief. Although it is straight exposition, there are descriptive details, action, use of the five senses, and emotion laced throughout this scene.

Compare the next two excerpts.

SHALLOW:

The <u>sadness</u> I <u>felt</u> <u>made</u> me waver on my feet. I didn't want to faint. When a huge wave of <u>depression</u> tugged at my heart, my thoughts turned back to the funeral.

The <u>grief</u> was overwhelming, as wind lifted the hair off my shoulders. My feet were <u>beginning to</u> hurt in my heels. My best friend was frozen beside me, a gloomy expression on her face.

Another shift in footing, and the sorrow blurred my vision. Wavering, I was sure I would fall over.

Suddenly, I felt two arms wrapped around my waist, pulling me backward against him. A nose touched just beneath my ear, and I could hear his deep breathing.

Trent was here. I wanted to turn and look at him, but only a huge sigh of misery shuddered through my body.

DEEP POV:

Tears choked my throat, burning as they threatened to bubble over and spill from my eyes. I wavered on my feet, sure I was going to faint like some attention seeking diva. With a cotton -filled head, my thoughts returned to the funeral unfolding before my disbelieving eyes. The body of my dad enclosed in a casket that was about to be lowered into the ground.

Sunlight bathed the graveyard in a warm blanket and a mild wind lifted the hair gently from my shoulders, like Dad's soft caress.

My feet were already hurting in my heels, but my best friend seemed rooted to the spot, an agonized expression fixed on her face. Ariana's fingers felt sweaty in my hand, but held mine steadfastly. Neither of us were willing to let each other go.

Another shift in footing, and my mind pulled down a protective screen of translucent gray silk across my line-of-sight. Wavering, I was sure I would find myself on the ground.

Suddenly, two strong arms wrapped around my waist, pulling me back into a solid wall of muscle. A nose buried in the crook beneath my ear, and his deep breathing ghosted along my skin.

Trent. He was here. Now. I wanted to turn and look at him, but slumped against him instead. A huge sigh shuddered through my body.

***

I hope these examples help you to revise your own stories.

EMOTION: WORRY

This chapter covers how to omit this common "telling" word from your writing: *concerned / worried / anxious*. Make sure that when you search for all of the words listed in this handbook in your own manuscript that you look for variations. For instance, if the word is "worry" then also search for *worried, worrying, upsetting, upset, distressing, distressed, fretting, fret,* etc.

Anytime a writer *names the emotion*, it takes them out of Deep POV. As I said before, you cannot revise every occurrence, but once you master this technique, you'll be able to eliminate shallow writing without stating the emotion the majority of the time.

Some physical signs of worry might be:

Face slackened

Brow furrowed

Eyes darting about in concern

Face looked pinched

Foot tapping

Unable to sleep or eat

Lip twitches

Blink excessively

Clamp and unclamp teeth

Face pales

Expression taut, drawn

Stomach clenches

Lick dry lips

Fidget

Bite nails

Examples of the emotion: WORRIED / WORRY.

SHALLOW: I was worried about Brandon being allergic to the new puppy.

DEEP POV: Biting my nails, I gazed into the puppy's cute little face. "If Brandon's allergic to you, I don't know what we'll do." The dog wagged his bushy tail in response.

SHALLOW: I <u>felt</u> <u>anxious</u> and <u>nervous</u> the night before my trip.

DEEP POV: Rubbing my sweaty hands on the thighs of my jeans, I double-checked that I had packed my passport and plane ticket for the hundredth time.

SHALLOW: He was <u>worried</u> that the birthday card had gotten lost in the mail.

DEEP POV: He still hadn't heard from his granddaughter about the card he'd mailed weeks ago. Eyebrows drawn together, he grabbed the phone to call her.

SHALLOW: I often <u>worry</u> about a zombie apocalypse.

DEEP POV: I ran a jerky hand through my hair as I watched the horror movie. What if there really was a zombie apocalypse? Would I be ready?

SHALLOW: The vampire <u>worried</u> that he'd drank too much of her blood.

DEEP POV: The vampire stepped back and wrung his hands. The girl's complexion paled to a ghostly white. He must've drunk just a little too much this time.

SHALLOW: I <u>felt</u> <u>apprehensive</u> the night before my wedding.

DEEP POV: Unable to sit still, I paced the hotel corridor. What if the caterer is late? What if the groom doesn't show up? Or worse…what if after eating that second slice of peach cobbler, I can't zip up my wedding dress?

SHALLOW: He was <u>concerned</u> about the accident on the road up ahead.

DEEP POV: His brow furrowed when he caught a glimpse of the accident on the road up ahead.

SHALLOW: Rachel <u>looked</u> <u>worried</u>.

DEEP POV: Rachel twisted a long strand of hair around her finger, and one leg bounced up and down.

SHALLOW: Cheri sighed, her expression <u>troubled</u>.

DEEP POV: Rubbing at a tic above her left eyebrow, Cheri sighed for the fiftieth time.

***

Next, I have a longer example to give you a better context of how to write in Deeper POV and avoid shallow writing.

SHALLOW:

I <u>noticed</u> that the guy <u>looked</u> really cute. His eyes <u>looked</u> blue. I was just about to interrupt the conversation when the guy cackled at something the boy next to him said. He laughed long and hard. I moved away, <u>worried</u> that he might be losing his mind. It was the most appalling <u>sound</u> I'd ever <u>heard</u>.

When he finally stopped laughing and started walking away, I felt too nervous to speak to him. But as he passed me by, I got a good look at his orange complexion.

I looked at my friends, baffled.

"Do you think he was wearing makeup?" Jessica asked worriedly.

"Maybe one of those spray-on tans," I said. "How shallow can he be?"

"I know," Amber said, giggling.

DEEP POV:

Damn, that guy was cute. His eyes sparkled like aquamarines. I was just about to tap his shoulder and introduce myself when the hottie chuckled at something his buddy had said. Hooted, actually. His laughter exploding all over the place like a crazy hyena. He doubled over with both hands on his knees and sucked in air with panting gasps.

What was wrong with this guy?

I shuffled backward. Sheesh, he was going to have a seizure at any moment. His horrible sounding giggles were the goofiest and most immature noise on the planet.

He finally straightened and sauntered out of the room with his friend, still wheezing.

As he passed by me, I got a very up close and personal glimpse of his "tan" skin. The fake color was virtually orange.

I glanced at my friends with an "oh-my-god-did-you-see-that?" expression.

Jessica stifled a giggle with one hand. "Was he wearing makeup?"

"More like one of those spray-on tans you can get at the mall," I said, rolling my eyes. "How superficial can that guy be?"

Amber shook her head with a giggle. "I know, right?"

***

I sincerely hope that all of my examples help you to revise your own work.

EMOTION: FEAR

In Deep POV, a writer gets straight to the point by describing the emotion instead of bluntly stating it. As with most writing rules, exceptions do exist, but only if using the filter word will cause the sentence structure to read more smoothly. However, in most cases, a quick rewrite can almost always fix shallower writing into Deeper POV.

For example, try to omit using words like: *fear / afraid / terrified / terror/ dread / fright / trepidation / apprehension / scared* from your writing.

Some physical signs of fear might be:

Skin becomes clammy

Voice becomes high and hysterical

Screaming

Sweat prickling scalp

Pulse speeds up

A rush of blood through head

A weight seems to press on chest

Body pumps out adrenaline

Hands get sweaty

Hyperventilate

Trembling hands

Brows drew together

Body shaking

Little hairs prickling on the back of the neck

Teeth chattering

Examples of the emotion: FEAR

SHALLOW: I feel a brief thrill of fear.

DEEP POV: Trembles travel from my legs and vibrate up my neck.

SHALLOW: She was paralyzed with fear. (Cliché)

DEEP POV: She couldn't move. Until that fight-or-flight response kicked in, begging her to run into the house and lock the door.

SHALLOW: <u>Terror</u> whooshed up and around him like waves.

DEEP POV: His heart was beating at a dizzying pace.

SHALLOW: <u>Terror</u> shot through me.

DEEP POV: My heart thudded louder and louder.

SHALLOW: He was <u>afraid</u> of the dark.

DEEP POV: Staring into the utter darkness, his palms grew damp.

SHALLOW: She was <u>terrified</u> of spiders.

DEEP POV: Her hair caught in a sticky web and she yelped. *Sheesh, I hate spiders!*

SHALLOW: She <u>felt a growing sense of dread</u>. (Cliché)

DEEP POV: A weight seemed to press on her chest, robbing her of breath.

SHALLOW: Katie was <u>frightened</u> by the loud screams.

DEEP POV: Loud screams split the night air. Katie's face turned ashen.

SHALLOW: A sliver of <u>apprehension</u> <u>made</u> her legs wobble.

DEEP POV: Walking stiffly toward the door, her knees locked and she wobbled.

SHALLOW: A sense of <u>dread</u> crept into her heart. (Cliché)

DEEP POV: All the blood drained from her face and her heart thudded hard.

SHALLOW: <u>Terror</u> welled up in his eyes. (Cliché)

DEEP POV: His eyes bulged from their sockets and he started to hyperventilate.

SHALLOW: Tendrils of <u>terror</u> curled into her stomach.

DEEP POV: Her stomach turned to ice and she steadied herself against the car.

SHALLOW: Zack <u>felt</u> the <u>fear</u> clench like a tight first around his chest.

DEEP POV: Zach's chest tightened like a clenched first around his chest.

SHALLOW: The <u>trepidation</u> in her voice <u>caused</u> him to become <u>apprehensive</u>.

DEEP POV: Her tone sounded so ominous that cold sweat trickled down his sides.

***

This longer excerpt is taken from my adult paranormal romance novel IMMORTAL ECLIPSE, and it shows how to portray *fear* effectively in your writing.

Remember that *every* word choice is vital to characterization and to making your writing style unique, so pick strong verbs. For emphasis, I underlined the filter words below in the shallow example.

SHALLOW:

At the <u>sound</u> of the thump, I <u>touch</u> the gun under my pillow. A girl like me living alone in New York must be careful. My fingers <u>feel</u> clumsy as I slide the safety off. Sudden <u>fear</u> chokes my throat.

I sit up slowly, and <u>feel</u> my body tense up. An eerie sensation batters my senses. Beneath my ribs, I <u>can feel</u> inside my heart, an alien power stir. The <u>feeling</u> is strange, but makes me <u>feel</u> clearheaded. The <u>feeling</u> buzzes over my skin. I try to swallow, but the lump of <u>dread</u> in my throat won't let me.

Then I <u>hear</u> a scraping <u>sound</u>.

I switch on the bedside lamp, and light illuminates the room. I get to my feet and look at the closed bedroom door in <u>terror</u>. The hardwood floor <u>feels</u> icy, and I <u>can feel</u> the spread of <u>panic</u>.

The scratching <u>sound</u> comes from under the door, <u>sounding</u> like fingernails on a chalkboard. With growing <u>fear</u> rising in my heart, I move toward the door. A board groans under my foot and I <u>feel</u> a fresh wave of <u>terror</u>.

The blinds are pulled up, making me <u>feel</u> defenseless. Beyond the street lamps, I <u>can see</u> lights glow in the towering skyscrapers and winds bend the trees. I <u>feel</u> the brownstone shift on its foundation.

I <u>hear</u> that scraping <u>sound</u> again.

I <u>think</u> it might be an animal or neighbor making those scary <u>sounds</u>.

An airstream moves through the room. It's scary and fills me with <u>dread</u>. That weird psychic <u>feeling</u> kicks up my <u>anxiety</u> a notch.

***

The next example shows more "voice," action, and emotion by using the Deep POV method. And effectively illustrates how to convey *fear* in your character without *naming the emotion*.

DEEP POV:

At the next ominous thump, I finger the handle of the Glock 19 under my pillow. My heart thunders. A girl living alone in New York must be careful, even in the Upper East Side. My fingers are clumsy and moist as I slide the safety off, the cold metal heavy in my hand.

Whoever's trying to break into my apartment had better think twice.

I sit up slowly, listening hard. My body tenses. An eerie sensation batters my senses, like a sixth sense awakening, blooming, and soaking through my bones. As it intensifies, the sense of urgency clears any traces of drowsiness. I try to swallow, but the lump in my throat won't let me.

This isn't the first time I've felt such a sensation, but right now it's off the charts. My weird intuition often shows up right before I bump into an old friend, someone knocks on my door, or a phone rings. Or worse, when I'm about to find myself knee -deep in trouble. My own personal warning device.

Scrape, scrape, scrape.

The thumping noise is replaced by a scratching on the other side of the apartment. It unnervingly echoes like fingernails grating down a chalkboard. The building responds, crooning under a blanket of wind.

I fumble to switch on the bedside lamp, and soft white light illuminates the room. Staggering to my feet, I stare at the closed bedroom door.

Scrape, scrape, scrape.

Hunching my shoulders, I take a tentative step closer. The hardwood floor is icy, and gooseflesh rises stiff and fast on my arms. I move again, tiptoeing toward the door. A board groans sharply under my weight.

So much for being quiet.

Scrape, scrape, scrape.

Could it be an animal making those noises? A neighbor?

A sudden draft moves through the room. It's reminiscent of sticky breath laden with foul odors, close and oppressive. That weird psychic sensation hits hard again, and it feels as though I've locked myself in a dark closet with a hundred vipers.

***

Could you tell the huge difference between the two examples?

The first one is cluttered with filter words that caused narrative distance and described the emotions. However, the second example gets the reader in close and personal because it is written in Deeper POV, so that the reader can really experience the fear in the character as she moves through her apartment.

EMOTION: UNEASE

Other filter words that create shallow writing and take you out of Deep POV are *uneasy, unease, uneasiness, panic, panicked, unnerved, rattled,* etc.

Most stories will become a page-turning read if you consider revising any shallow writing that takes you out of Deep POV. So I suggest finding ways to revise any "telling" scenes so that they come alive for the reader. Try to be ruthless and revise these filter words in your own WIP.

Some physical signs of panic can be:

Clutching at collar of shirt

Wringing shirt tightly

Lacing fingers taut until knuckles turn white

Loss of appetite

Heart feels like it drops into stomach

Nervous tics: fidgeting or rubbing forehead

Cannot relax

Mentally obsessing over problem

Rubbing (wiping) sweaty hands down thigh repeatedly

Grinding teeth

Tense jaw

Staring off into space

Unable to sleep

Feel like crying

Eye twitching

Examples of the emotion: Panic/ Unease

SHALLOW: Her <u>panic</u> level shot sky-high.

DEEP POV: She stumbled backward, bumping into a chair.

SHALLOW: A <u>feeling</u> of <u>panic</u> skittered up my spine. (Cliché)

DEEP POV: A cold tremor shot down my back.

SHALLOW: The tiny seeds of her eyes showed <u>unease</u>.

DEEP POV: Grinding her teeth, she blinked rapidly. *No!*

SHALLOW: <u>Panic</u> <u>made</u> my stomach nauseous and I <u>noticed</u> my hands shook.

DEEP POV: My stomach was queasy and my hands wouldn't stop shaking.

SHALLOW: <u>Anxiety</u> overcame me when I checked my bank statement.

DEEP POV: Clutching tightly at the collar of my shirt, I stared at the zeros on my bank statement.

SHALLOW: Dan experienced a moment of body-numbing <u>panic</u>.

DEEP POV: Clenching his hands into tight fists, Dan's body went numb.

SHALLOW: I <u>felt</u> a huge bubble of <u>panic</u> build in my chest.

DEEP POV: Lacing my fingers taut until my knuckles turned white, I tried to remain calm.

SHALLOW: The whole idea of high school dances gave me <u>anxiety</u>.

DEEP POV: I shuddered. High school dances sucked.

SHALLOW: I look <u>anxiously</u> around the cabin.

DEEP POV: Mouth dry and heartbeat racing, I glance about the cabin.

SHALLOW: Maria shot Alexander a <u>panicked</u> look.

DEEP POV: Maria's body twitched and she faced Alexander with wide-open eyes.

***

Most scenes can be even more emotional, vivid, and visual if you try to go deeper with the five senses and include physical sensations. Consider revising your WIP by finding ways to make each scene more visceral and powerful through the Deep POV technique.

EMOTION: NERVOUSNESS

In order for our readers to experience emotions right alongside our characters, they must feel what the character feels at any given moment in your novel or short story. But contrary to suspense, and the way many of us write, we *name the emotion* that the character is experiencing instead of describing it.

"Telling" the reader only achieves the opposite effect of Deeper POV. So, try to exclude shallow words like *nervous, anxious, concerned, apprehensive, fretful, fearful, panicky, uneasy,* from your scenes.

Some physical signs of anxiety might be:

Facial tics or spasms

Toes curl

Voice wavers / rises an octave

Shift nervously in chair

Hands intertwined with each other repeatedly

Constant fidgeting

Tapping of the foot

Limited eye contact

Talking fast

Trembling voice or stuttering

Sweat beading on forehead

Clenched fists to stop them from trembling

Eyes unfocused

Face pale

Stomach bile in throat

Examples of the emotion: NERVOUSNESS

SHALLOW: Piper <u>felt</u> <u>nervous</u> about the contest.

DEEP POV: Piper broke out in a cold sweat whenever she thought of the contest.

SHALLOW: A bout of <u>nervousness</u> struck Kent.

DEEP POV: Rubbing the back of his neck, Kent shifted his weight from one foot to the other.

SHALLOW: A <u>nervous</u> <u>feeling</u> stayed with Jamie all day.

DEEP POV: Jamie closed her eyes and took a calming breath, but it was no use.

SHALLOW: I <u>felt</u> <u>nervous</u> butterflies in my stomach. (Cliché)

DEEP POV: My hands trembled in my lap. My stomach pitched and rolled.

SHALLOW: Claire was too <u>nervous</u> to eat dinner.

DEEP POV: Claire pushed the food around on her plate without taking so much as a bite.

SHALLOW: I <u>felt</u> overly <u>anxious</u> that night.

DEEP POV: I was a bundle of raw nerves that night, my muscles twitchy.

SHALLOW: The closer we got to Grandma's house, the more <u>nervous</u> I became.

DEEP POV: As Grandma's house loomed ahead of us, my pulse quickened.

SHALLOW: Her stomach clenched with <u>nervousness</u>.

DEEP POV: Bile rose in her throat and her stomach clenched.

SHALLOW: Spencer looked visibly <u>nervous</u>.

DEEP POV: Her gaze darted around the room and she jumped at every sound.

SHALLOW: I shifted my weight <u>nervously</u>.

DEEP POV: I shifted my weight, my leg muscles quivering.

***

Sometimes it is okay to leave the "telling" word in a sentence, but I would advise for Deeper POV to at least try to weed any filter words from your narrative. If you read a ton of fiction like me, you'll notice "telling" words in almost every published novel, some more than others, but that doesn't mean *you* should do it in your own writing.

Here is another example of how to avoid *naming the emotion*.

SHALLOW:

I stood in the doorway and my heart started to beat fast. I felt really nervous. I wondered if the students would notice my rising anxiety.

From the entrance, I saw seven grinning faces staring back at me. They fell quiet as soon as Hunter moved past me into the room. I gulped, my panicked nerves singing.

Hunter faced the kids. "Hey guys, this is the new teacher's aide, Mrs. Beckman—"

"It's only Miss Beckman," I said loudly. "I'm unmarried."

DEEP POV:

I dragged my size nine feet into the noisy classroom and my heart beat erratically. I wrung my hands on my already wrinkled polyester turtleneck. My body broke out in a light sweat as I glanced around the room.

Is it hot in here or is it just me?

I shuffled across the threshold and seven smiley faces turned toward the doorway. They fell quiet as soon as Hunter shouldered past me into the room. I gulped. Loudly.

Hunter faced the students. "Hey guys, this is the new teacher's aide, Mrs. Beckman—"

"It's *Miss* Beckman," I interrupted, my face flushing hot. "I'm not, um, married."

***

Hope all of these examples from my own stories spark your creative muse!

EMOTION: RELIEF

The "telling" word *relief/relieved* can weaken your writing. This emotion is often stated in books and the manuscripts that I edit, but it is considered shallow writing.

And please don't rely too heavily on overused clichés like "he sighed with relief." Most clichés like this have been so stereotyped that now they sound weak and boring.

Some physical signs of relief might be:

Shoulders relax

Closing eyes and sighing

Mumbling a prayer of thanks

Sighing loudly

Tension in body diminishing

One hand over chest / heart

Body sags against wall

Throw head back

Wide smile

Clapping hands

Standing straighter

Muscles unwind

Breathing out / exhaling

Hugging other people

Tears cloud eyes

Examples of the emotion: RELIEF

SHALLOW: Relief flooded her system. (Cliché)

DEEP POV: Shaking her head and closing her eyes, her body relaxed.

SHALLOW: Locating an empty seat on the bus, I plopped down with a rush of relief.

DEEP POV: Locating the last empty seat on the bus, I plopped down and smiled. *Ha!* Lucky me.

SHALLOW: I exhaled with a small measure of relief. (Cliché)

DEEP POV: Sagging against a wall, the tension in my shoulders dissolved.

SHALLOW: Tommy <u>felt</u> a little wave of <u>relief</u>.

DEEP POV: Tommy pressed his palm to his heart and the fast beating slowed.

SHALLOW: He sighed in <u>relief</u>.

DEEP POV: With tears brimming his eyes, he exhaled. *We were safe now.*

SHALLOW: <u>Relief</u> trickled through her veins.

DEEP POV: Softly thanking God, she closed her eyes and sighed.

SHALLOW: I breathed a sigh of <u>relief</u>. (Cliché)

DEEP POV: A sudden lightness struck my senses. Everything was going to be okay after all.

SHALLOW: Cat nearly sobbed with <u>relief</u>.

DEEP POV: Exhaling loudly, Cat swallowed the emotion.

SHALLOW: She'd been <u>relieved</u> that yesterday's fight hadn't ended in a horrible breakup.

DEEP POV: The tension left her body. Yesterday's fight wasn't that big of a deal and it hadn't resulted in a horrible breakup.

SHALLOW: At first, I'd thought he was completely undressed, but I was relieved to see the navy boxer shorts.

DEEP POV: At first glance, his bare torso gleamed in the dim light. *Holy smokes! He's naked.* Another peek revealed a pair of sexy navy boxer shorts. *Whew.*

***

Here are two paragraphs, one is *telling* and the other is *showing*. The first one has too many filter words and overworked clichés.

SHALLOW:

Noel was so relieved that she'd passed the exam that she practically jumped for joy. She stepped outside the classroom and it felt like a weight had been lifted off her chest. As she hurried down the steps, her heart felt lighter.

***

The next example has been revised into Deep POV, and it *shows* the emotion without bluntly stating it for the reader.

DEEP POV:

A slow smile touches Noel's lips. *She'd done it!* Aced that exam.

She practically skipped out of the classroom, humming happily to herself. She hurried down the steps and hopped into her car. Her head fell back against the headrest and her grin widened. Time to celebrate.

***

These examples should give you some clear-cut ideas on how to revise your own manuscript into Deep POV.

EMOTION: SURPRISE

A lot of new writers and published authors often name this emotion *shock, surprise, amazement, amazed, stunned, dazed* rather than describe it. I've done it in my own novels, too. However, it is always better to *show* rather than *tell* as discussed in this handbook.

Some physical signs of surprise might be:

Gawk at someone

Mouth fall open

Eyes go wide

Hands flying to cover mouth

Eyebrows raised

Stare unblinking

Short harsh gasps

Nervous laughter

Facial muscles twitch

Cheeks blush

Stagger backward

Inhale sharply

Mouth moving wordlessly

Jaw dropping

Examples of the emotion: SHOCK / SURPRISE

SHALLOW: He was <u>shocked</u> by her outburst. (Cliché)

DEEP POV: Squeezing his eyes shut, he rubbed his temples.

SHALLOW: Remy watched us, looking as <u>surprised</u>.

DEEP POV: Remy stared at us with her mouth gaping open like a fish on a hook.

SHALLOW: Ally was <u>surprised</u> by Haley's confession.

DEEP POV: Ally didn't know what to say as the blood drained out of her face.

SHALLOW: Dean wore a look of <u>shock</u>.

DEEP POV: Dean's face paled and he grabbed his brother's arm to steady himself.

SHALLOW: Missy turned red with <u>astonishment</u>.

DEEP POV: Missy gaped, a fluttery feeling striking her belly.

SHALLOW: He reacted with <u>shocked</u> concern.

DEEP POV: Spreading his fingers out in a fan against his breastbone, Jake swore under his breath.

SHALLOW: I looked at Luke with a little <u>surprise</u>.

DEEP POV: My breath hitched in my throat when I looked at Luke. No way could zombies be real.

SHALLOW: I jerked in <u>surprise</u>.

DEEP POV: My body jerked and I dug my fingers into my palms.

SHALLOW: I was <u>shocked</u> into silence by his confession.

DEEP POV: Both of my hands flew up to cover my mouth.

SHALLOW: She <u>looked surprised</u> when he touched her arm, as if she'd forgotten Bradly was there.

DEEP POV: Cheeks flaming, she took a startled step back. She'd forgotten Bradly was still there until he touched her elbow.

***

Here is another much longer example on how to revise your own work from shallow writing into vivid Deeper POV.

SHALLOW:

I was <u>shocked</u> and <u>surprised</u> that Janet had actually come today. She didn't even dress for gym half the time.

Cheerleading tryouts had been ruthless, and as team captain, I <u>knew</u> that I had a tough choice to make. It was either my best friend, Bria, or the bigger girl, Janet.

Coach Malkin <u>looked</u> at me. "Who's it gonna be, Lacy? You have to pick either Janet or Bria."

"I'm not really sure," I said and bent down to tie the laces on my sneakers. "Do I have to decide right now?"

"Well, I can make the decision for you," Coach said with a <u>look of concern</u>.

"Okay," I said, <u>brightening</u> and hoping it would be my BFF.

Come on! I <u>thought</u>. *Pick Bria!*

"Bria Harvey," Coach announced.

"Yes!" I shouted loudly.

After a <u>stunned</u> silence, everyone broke out into quiet laughter.

<u>Embarrassment</u> flushed my face, but I couldn't stop the wide smile.

DEEP POV:

Cheerleading tryouts had been brutal, and as team captain, I had a tough choice to make.

Why had Big-Hipped-Janet even showed up today?

Her chubby cheeks were red and sweat ran down her face. Janet leaned over, panting hard like a dog. She was uncoordinated and at least twenty pounds heavier than the other girls.

It was down to my *very* thin best friend, Bria, or overweight Janet, who was nice, but would be impossible to lift.

Coach Malkin glanced over at me with a raised brow. "Well, Lacy...who's it gonna be? Janet or Bria?"

"Um...yeah...well...I'm not really sure," I mumbled and bent down to retie the laces on my ultra white Stretchers. "Do I have to decide today?"

"If you can't choose, it's all right. I can make the decision for you," Coach said softly and squeezed my shoulder.

"Okay," I said and a small smile lifted my lips.

Come on! Pick my BFF! Bria, Bria, Bria...

"Bria Harvey."

"Yay!" I jumped up out of my seat, clapping my hands.

The entire squad stared at me for a full minute of awkward silence, and then everyone laughed.

Oops. Guess that was a little bit melodramatic, even for me.

My face turned fire engine red, but I couldn't stop grinning like an idiot. Bria had made the team!

***

Now you should have even more insight and knowledge on how to revise your manuscript into page-turning prose.

EMOTION: CONFUSION

This chapter will offer some helpful examples of how to rewrite your sentences from "telling" into showing by eliminating the shallow words *confused / confusion / doubt* from your narrative.

Showing the cause-effect connection is critical when expressing true emotions. But I recommend that you never state the emotion.

Some physical signs of confusion or doubt might be:

Nose scrunched up

Eyebrows knitted together

Staring sightlessly

Unsettling feeling

Hesitate to respond

Briskly shaking head

Licking lips

Tip head to the side

Ask someone to repeat information

Frown deeply

Scrunched up expression

Wrinkled forehead

Scratching head

Blank look on face

Twitching lips

Examples of the emotion: CONFUSION

SHALLOW: She was so <u>confused</u> by Hunter's story.

DEEP POV: She scrunched her eyebrows and tilted her head to the side. "Huh? I don't understand."

SHALLOW: He <u>felt</u> utterly <u>confused</u> by the group's announcement.

DEEP POV: He looked from one person to another, with a blank expression on his face. *He didn't get the job?*

SHALLOW: She was <u>perplexed</u> and <u>bewildered</u> by this turn of events.

DEEP POV: Her eyes grew wide. She opened and closed her mouth, but no words leaked from her twitching lips.

SHALLOW: She looked confused and upset by the news.

DEEP POV: She shook her head and wet her lips. "Are you serious?"

SHALLOW: I stare at him in confusion.

DEEP POV: My stomach pitches. I'm unable to digest the words. *Is he really breaking up with me?*

SHALLOW: Feeling puzzled, I gaped at Jessie in confusion.

DEEP POV: I tugged hard on my earlobe and swallowed several times before I could speak again. "Are you sure it was my mom, Jessie?"

SHALLOW: I blinked in confusion. (Cliché)

DEEP POV: I blinked rapidly. My nerves jangled. *Was he for real?*

SHALLOW: Cole's harsh tone left me even more confused.

DEEP POV: Slumping onto a seat, I tried to figure out why Cole was upset.

SHALLOW: I was perplexed by the cat's hissing.

DEEP POV: I shook my head. What the heck was that cat hissing at now?

SHALLOW: My brows furrowed in confusion. (Cliché)

DEEP POV: Blowing out a breath, I stared at him.

***

It is okay to use the word *confused / confusion* at times in a scene; however, you can use it more effectively in dialogue instead of stating it in the narrative. Or if the main character is noticing the emotion in another character. But it is always so much more powerful to be *shown*.

Here is a longer example to illustrate how effective Deep POV can be if you use this method to describe the emotion instead of just stating it.

This excerpt is taken from book one, BEAUTIFULLY BROKEN. The first version is crammed with shallow writing. However, the second is a good example of how to describe *confusion* without *naming the emotion*, and it blends "voice" with emotion, dialogue, and action.

SHALLOW:

"Really?" I asked in <u>confusion</u>. "Because he didn't seem too interested when Brittany was stalking him at church on Sunday."

Brittany didn't respond, but gave me a hard look. I <u>heard</u> Heather and Elesha snicker. I <u>thought</u> that Heather wasn't as tall as Elesha.

Then I <u>noticed</u> that Elesha had flawless dark brown skin and an athletic body. With her chestnut hair and a thick fringe of bangs framing her angular face, tight-fitting plaid skirt, and blazer, Heather looked overdressed.

"What do you know, freak?" Heather stepped closer and seized my upper arm. I <u>felt</u> her nails in my flesh. I <u>felt</u> her mouth near my ear, her words very cold <u>sounding</u>. "Let me clue you in: guys like Trent Donovan only date girls like *us*." She let go of my arm.

"Oh, yeah? Well, what if I told you he was smiling at me on Sunday?" I lied. <u>Feeling</u> <u>uneasy</u>, I wanted to take the words back.

"I'd say he was just being polite," Brittany said rudely. "Because I've got a date with him tonight."

I felt <u>nervous</u>. My face scrunched into <u>confused</u> lines.

A spark of <u>jealousy</u> boiled my insides. My skin bristled with <u>hate</u>. A strange energy—magickal power—stirred within me. I <u>felt</u> it heat my flesh and flow into my fingers, blending with my <u>anger</u>. It awakened something within me. Then I <u>noticed</u> a dark force gnawing to get out.

DEEP POV:

"Really?" My whole body tensed, muscles quivering. "Because he didn't seem too interested when Brittany was stalking him at church on Sunday."

Brittany stayed quiet, but gave me the stink eye. Heather and Elesha snickered. Heather wasn't as tall as Elesha, who had flawless dark brown skin and an athletic body. With her chestnut hair and a thick fringe of bangs framing her angular face, her gold hoop earrings, tight-fitting plaid skirt, and blazer, Heather looked ultra-preppy and runway ready.

I tried not to roll my eyes. She was attending public school, not a fashion show.

"What do you know, freak?" Heather took two steps and seized my upper arm. Her nails dug into my flesh. Her mouth was next to my ear, her words cold and clear as ice water. "Let me clue you in: guys like Trent Donovan only date girls like *us*. Girls who know how to show a guy a good time. We're *it* at this school. What would he see in a loser like you?" She let go of my arm.

"Oh, yeah? Well, what if I told you he was crazy smiling at me on Sunday? Huh?" I lied.

The words flew out of my mouth before I could think. Maybe I was growing a backbone after all.

"I'd say he was just being polite," Brittany replied. "Because I've got a date with him tonight."

My stomach flipped over hard. What? My forehead scrunched up as I stared at her. Trent and Brittany? *No effing way.*

My insides boiled. My skin bristled. A strange energy—magickal power—stirred within me like a dangerous live wire. It heated my flesh and flowed into my fingers, blending with my anger. It awakened something within me. A dark force gnawing to get out.

***

It is usually better when writing a conflicted main character to show the internal struggle through action, dialogue, and emotion like I did in my second example. By using Deep POV, the character will naturally convey their true feelings to the reader.

Well, I sincerely hope these examples help you to revise, revise, revise!

EMOTION: HAPPINESS

This chapter will cover how to show *happiness / joy* without actually stating the emotion for the reader. I'm not saying you cannot use this descriptive word if it is appropriate, but if you revise a scene without *naming the emotion*, your work will come alive for the reader.

Some physical signs of happiness might be:

Eyes sparkling

Feeling of lightness

Bouncing on toes

Swinging arms

Explosion of endorphins

Laughing / giggling

Heart swelling

Hugging yourself

Skin glows

Cheering and squealing

Hyper aware of surroundings

Full of energy

Lighthearted / playful

Singing or humming to yourself

Voice high-pitched / excited

Examples of the emotion: HAPPINESS / JOY

SHALLOW: A flood of <u>happiness</u> poured through me. (Cliché)

DEEP POV: Swinging my arms while walking home, I couldn't stop grinning.

SHALLOW: She was so <u>happy</u> that she'd won the new car.

DEEP POV: Bouncing on her toes, she clutched the keys to her new car in one hand. "This is the best day of my life!" she exclaimed and hugged the stranger standing next to her.

SHALLOW: Elizabeth wanted to jump for <u>joy</u>. (Cliché)

DEEP POV: Holding both of her arms out wide as if she could hug the entire world, Elizabeth beamed at her husband. A second honeymoon sounded awesome.

SHALLOW: A sense of <u>joy</u> bubbled up in her heart.

DEEP POV: A sense of weightlessness struck her heart. She rubbed her cheeks, her face hurting from the wide grin that lifted her lips.

SHALLOW: "That's great news!" I cried <u>happily</u>.

DEEP POV: If my smile became any wider, I'd resemble the Joker. "Great news!"

SHALLOW: Sandy actually squealed in <u>happiness</u>.

DEEP POV: "Yay!" Sandy giggled uncontrollably and clapped her hands. "Let's party!"

SHALLOW: I <u>felt</u> <u>happy</u> when Sam told me the good news.

DEEP POV: A big goofy grin pulled at my mouth when Sam told me the good news.

SHALLOW: I'd never <u>felt</u> so <u>happy</u> to see the first rays of dawn in my life.

DEEP POV: As the first rays of dawn peeked through the blinds, I threw my arms wide.

SHALLOW: I sighed with true <u>happiness</u>.

DEEP POV: A sigh escaped and I beamed.

SHALLOW: I thought I might just die from <u>happiness</u>. (Cliché)

DEEP POV: Dancing around wildly, a bubbly sensation filled my heart.

***

This longer example shows you how to revise your "telling" sentences into *showing* through Deep POV. Again, it is fine to occasionally use the words *joy / happiness* in your writing, but if it's possible not to—then don't.

SHALLOW:

Damon wrapped his arms around me, and then I <u>felt</u> him put his lips to mine. I <u>felt</u> a thrill of profound <u>happiness</u> as Damon stroked my back. I <u>felt</u> my heartbeat quicken.

But Damon wasn't a very good kisser. Maybe my friend Mindy could provide some instruction.

Damon pulled back. "I'll call you later, okay?"

I <u>realized</u> I had his slobber on my chin. "Sure." I stood there <u>watching</u> as the pickup drove away.

When the taillights had almost vanished into the darkness, I <u>headed</u> toward the porch. I <u>felt</u> my heart lift with <u>joy,</u> even though I <u>knew</u> the kiss had been awful.

***

I have included "voice," emotion, and dialogue in my next example to give you a better idea of how to redraft scenes in your own work.

DEEP POV:

Damon wrapped his arms around my waist and pulled me closer. My breath hitched in my throat. For a moment, a warm thrill shot through my body when his soft lips touched mine.

Yuk. Too sloppy.

But hopefully this kissing stuff would get better with lots and lots of practice. Maybe I could borrow Mindy's book on *Twenty-Five Ways to Be a Great Lover.* That girl had to be a professional, the way she was always practicing her kissing techniques on her pillow.

Damon pulled back and smiled. "I gotta get going. Call you later, okay?"

Trying not to act grossed out that his slobber was wetting my chin, I said, "Yeah. Sure."

I grinned like a big doofus until the truck pulled away. When the taillights faded into the night, I skipped onto the porch, swirling the hem of my skirt back and forth like a little girl.

Wow. *My first real kiss.* What a disaster! But also all kinds of awesome.

***

Now I challenge you to rewrite a scene in your own novel or story where the characters experience true happiness and *show* it.

EMOTION: JEALOUSLY

In almost every scene, I think it's important to stay in Deep POV. As you revise, remember that there are a dozen different ways to describe a physical, internal, or emotional response. By filtering the "telling" words throughout your narrative, you'll discover some interesting things about your characters.

For example, if you can eliminate the "telling" words *jealousy, envy, envious, wariness, mistrustfulness, resentment, resentfulness, spite, begrudge* from your narrative, then you'll stay in Deeper POV.

Some physical signs of envy might be:

Breath harsh and shallow

Hands curling into fists at sides

Teeth clenched

Chest puffs out / heats up

Heart lurches

Burning sensation in chest

Wanting to cry

Crossing arms

Tight muscles

Quick toss of head

Voice low, snarky

Body tenses up

Pain in heart area

Face reddens

Neck grows hot

Examples of the emotion: JEALOUSY

SHALLOW: Darren was green with <u>jealousy</u>. (Cliché)

DEEP POV: Shoving the hair from his eyes, Darren stomped inside the house. The nerve of Tom flashing his new lawnmower in front of all the neighbors. But damn, that machine was cool looking.

SHALLOW: A spark of <u>jealousy</u> struck my heart.

DEEP POV: A pang struck my heart. How could Krystal buy the same dress I'd been drooling over for weeks? And the gown looked better on her than me.

SHALLOW: There was an edge of jealousy in my own voice.

DEEP POV: Clenching my teeth, I snapped, "I always *knew* you liked her better!"

SHALLOW: I tried very hard not to envy her.

DEEP POV: My best friend was beyond spoiled. New car. Expensive apartment. Trust fund. And she took it all for granted while I slaved away working double-shifts for minimum wage.

SHALLOW: Feeling a stab of envy, Christina glared at Yolanda.

DEEP POV: A burning sensation stabbed Christina in the chest. Yolanda thought she was *so* special with her new haircut and designer purse. Ha! That bag was a cheap knockoff and she'd prove it.

SHALLOW: I can't contain my envy.

DEEP POV: My eyes narrow. My breaths come out coarser as I stare down at the gifts under the lighted tree. *So unfair!* Jonathon always got ten times more Christmas presents than me.

SHALLOW: I felt jealousy growing inside me.

DEEP POV: Huffing, I tried to contain the green monster growling inside me, but failed. "Your book is on the bestseller's list *again?*" I spat. Mine hadn't even made *Amazon's Top 100*.

SHALLOW: Hot <u>jealousy</u> colored her dark tone.

DEEP POV: Her ugly tone luridly colored her accusation and I half-expected her breath to come out in little green puffs.

SHALLOW: Dean's <u>jealous</u> grip on me tightened. "Are you cheating on me?"

DEEP POV: Dean's grip tightened on my arm and his neck muscles bunched up. "Are you cheating on me?"

SHALLOW: <u>Envy</u> oozed from him in waves when he <u>saw</u> his ex with another man.

DEEP POV: His chest puffed out and his movements stiffened when he spotted his ex with that tall dude.

***

In this next illustration, I show how using deeper narration and vivid emotion allows you to effectively turn your shallow scene into Deeper POV scene.

SHALLOW:

I <u>felt</u> my throat crowd with <u>jealousy</u>. There was something wrong with me. I had my own boyfriend, but I wanted to be with hers. I already <u>knew</u> Kyle was cute and sexy and nice. I <u>wished</u> that he'd seen me first.

"Wanna see another picture of Kyle at the beach?" Tamara asked sweetly.

"Sure," I said, jealousy tainting my voice.

She didn't notice as she scrolled to a photo of Kyle taken on her iPhone. I thought he looked very handsome in shorts and shirtless, his big smile, and his tousled dark hair.

My heart panged again with growing envy.

DEEP POV:

Pursing my lips into a flat, hard line, I tried to ignore the way my body flushed hot and cold. *What's wrong with me?*

My best friend was showing off pics of her hot new boyfriend, and instead of being happy for her, it made my own boyfriend seem like a boring nerd.

How selfish could I be?

"Wanna see another picture of Kyle at the beach?" Tamara asked with a smile.

No. I really, really *didn't* want to keep looking at photos of her perfect boyfriend.

Taking a step closer, fists clenched, I muttered, "Yeah...I guess."

Tamara smiled and handed me her iPhone. In the photo, Kyle looked insanely hot in board shorts with no shirt, his muscled chest sprinkled with water and his black hair tousled with ocean water.

Damn, he was a hottie. And unfortunately, all *hers*.

***

A good thing to remember as you revise a scene into Deeper POV is that male and female characters should react, experience, communicate, and convey feelings differently. When writing a character of the opposite sex in Deep POV, try to get a second opinion by a beta reader or critique partner to ensure that the male and female character reactions, responses, and emotions are written realistically.

EMOTION: EMBARRASSMENT

This chapter provides a few examples on how to avoid too much "telling" and it includes ways to show a character's embarrassing moments through Deep POV.

For each scene, identify the emotion that your character needs to *show* and think of different ways you can reinforce the character's emotions through both verbal and nonverbal communication. One way is to omit "telling" words like *embarrassed, embarrassment, self-conscious, ashamed, mortified, humiliated, humiliation, shame* from your writing.

Some physical signs of embarrassment might be:

Stomach roiling

Faintness

Feeling the urge to pee

Legs quivering

Swallowing hard

Voice squeaks

Glancing around at surroundings

Not making eye contact

Backing away or running away

Hiding face in hair

Leg bouncing

Tugging at eyebrow / earlobe

Fiddling with jewelry or sleeves

Breathing fast and heavy

Vision hazy

Examples of the emotion: EMBARRASSMENT

SHALLOW: Feeling embarrassed, I jerked back.

DEEP POV: Jerking back, my neck turned red and I was breathing hard.

SHALLOW: I was actually embarrassed that he wanted to display that kind of affection in plain view of everyone.

DEEP POV: My cheeks flushed pink. *PDA in the cafeteria?* No. Thanks.

SHALLOW: I was so <u>embarrassed</u> that I wanted to run and hide. (Cliché)

DEEP POV: If the ground opened up and swallowed me right now, I'd be a happy camper.

SHALLOW: "I'm not going!" she said, <u>embarrassed</u> to be treated like a child.

DEEP POV: "I'm not going!" she snapped, a bloom of heat staining her neck and ears. She was almost eighteen! Her parents couldn't keep treating her like a child.

SHALLOW: I tucked my hands under my butt, feeling <u>embarrassed</u>

DEEP POV: I tucked my fidgety hands under my butt.

SHALLOW: I looked at the ground in <u>embarrassment</u>.

DEEP POV: Staring at my feet, I worked to steady my own breathing.

SHALLOW: I got that squirmy, <u>embarrassed</u> feeling that awkward conversations with parents can bring about.

DEEP POV: I got a squirmy feeling in my gut and shifted in my seat. This conversation with my parents was gonna be all kinds of awkward.

SHALLOW: An <u>embarrassed</u> blush stained my cheeks.

DEEP POV: A hot flush stained my cheeks.

SHALLOW: I took a deep breath and held it, squelching a <u>humiliated</u> giggle.

DEEP POV: Taking a deep breath, I held it in to stifle the unwelcome giggle.

SHALLOW: <u>Embarrassed</u>, I muttered, "Aren't you going to kiss me good night?"

DEEP POV: My heartbeat turned unruly and my voice became husky. "Aren't you going to kiss me good night?"

SHALLOW: She looked down, <u>feeling</u> <u>embarrassed</u>, but he pulled her chin up, turning her head so that she met his eyes.

DEEP POV: She turned away, her collarbone hot, but he pulled her chin up, turning her head so that she met his eyes.

***

These next paragraphs are written in both Shallow POV and Deep POV to exemplify how to revise sentences, paragraphs, and scenes in your own work.

This excerpt is taken from my novel IMMORTAL ECLIPSE and the *shallow* example is an early draft before revision. The second example is written in the Deep POV method and has lots of "voice,'" which makes it an up close and personal experience for the reader. In this excerpt, the heroine is meeting the love interest for the first time.

SHALLOW:

As we stand there staring at each other, I feel a thrilling sensation in my body and now I feel confused. I look at the dark-haired man in the doorway, trying not to stare at his blue eyes. He is a very good-looking man, I tell myself.

The tall man turns and his eyes meet mine. I notice that he's dressed similar to the man in the portrait: a linen shirt under a black vest and he is wearing pants and boots. Although, he must be in his late twenties, I think he looks reserved and intimidating.

Matthew didn't mention a man like this living here, I thought.

The man shakes his head, and then clears his throat.

"I'm Gerard Blackwell's niece."

I feel embarrassed for staring so long at him. My words make the mortification even worse. I wish I could start over and introduce myself properly.

DEEP POV:

As we stand there staring at each other, a thrilling electric current courses through my body and short-circuits my brain. I blink several times at the dark-haired man standing in the doorway, trying not to stare at his eyes, an intense shade of blue. Damn, he's better looking than most of the male fashion models I've photographed.

Mr. Tall, Dark, and Yummy tilts his head and his eyes lock on mine. Even from a distance, I can tell he'll tower over me, and I'm no midget. He's even dressed similar to the man in the portrait: a soft, white linen shirt—bulging biceps stretching the fabric—under a black vest paired with snug pants and boots. Although, he appears to be only in his late twenties, he looks reserved and intimidating.

Conclusion: no sense of style, but still smoking hot.

Matthew didn't mention anyone like *him* living on the property. Having eye candy like Matt around will be a nice distraction. The hottie regains his composure and clears his throat.

Stop acting like a drooling idiot and speak to him!

"Hello. I'm, uh, Gerard Blackwell's niece."

My face heats. That was brilliant. Great first impression. I could really, really use a do-over so I don't come across as an ogling idiot.

***

As you revise your own work, strive to look for the simplest clarification to remove the sensory "telling" words from your sentences and replace those offenders with Deep POV.

CONCLUSION

Now that you have a clearer idea on how to revise shallow scenes by using the Deep POV technique, here is a list of filter words that weren't mentioned in this handbook, but you should be aware of them.

Search for these "telling" words and revise your sentences by applying this amazing technique and it will take your writing skills to the next level.

Agitated

Alarmed

Ambivalent

Amused

Anguish

Annoyed

Ashamed

Bitter

Calm

Cautious

Cheerful

Compassion

Confident

Contempt

Content

Curious

Defeated

Defensive

Delighted

Desperate

Determined

Disgusted

Disillusioned

Dismayed

Disoriented

Distrust

Doubtful

Dread

Eager

Elated

Enthusiastic

Exhausted

Grateful

Grumpy

Guilty

Helpless

Hopeful or hopeless

Horrified

Hostile

Impatient

Inferior

Insecure

Insulted

Intrigued

Irritated

Isolated

Lonely

Nostalgic

Numb

Optimistic

Outraged

Overwhelmed

Paranoid

Pity

Proud

Regretful

Rejected

Reluctant

Remorseful

Resentful

Restless

Revulsion

Satisfied

Scornful

Shame

Skeptical

Smug

Spiteful

Stressed

Suspicious

Sympathetic

Vengeful

Wary

Weary

***

In closing, I strongly recommend that you begin studying more books on this wonderful editing method.

As the bestselling novelist Stephen King proclaims, *"If you don't have time to read, you don't have the time (or the tools) to write. Simple as that."*

One of the best ways to learn and strengthen your own writing talents is by observing how other published writers do it. Go to your local library, bookstore, or favorite online retailer to purchase a few books to read in Deep POV.

Recommended fiction reading:

Brandilyn Collins (Exposure)

Jill Elizabeth Nelson (Reluctant Burglar)

Melissa James (The Rebel King)

Rebecca Zanetti (Sweet Revenge)

J. D. Faver (On Ice)

Karen Ball (Any of her books)

And of course, Sherry Soule (All of my books)

Well, that concludes my advice on self-editing those annoying filter words and how to revise your wonderful story into Deeper POV.

Happy revising!

REQUEST

If you read this handbook and enjoyed the tools and tips of Deep POV, please consider posting an honest review on places like Amazon, Barnes & Noble, or Goodreads.

Indie novels would rarely reach the light of day without the dedication of readers willing to post a review. So please share the book love!

MORE EDITING TOOLS

Each of these helpful self-editing handbooks encompass many different topics such as, dialogue, exposition, character ARCs, setting, and other editing techniques that will help you take your writing to the next level!

Craft Vivid Scenes and Characters

Most writers struggle with constructing lifelike scenes and realistic character descriptions. This handbook offers tips on how to create vibrant settings and vivid characters that will deeply submerge the reader into the story. This handbook also provides vital techniques on world-building and character depictions, with bonus examples on how to combine the five senses and use Deep POV in all of your scenes, which will take your writing skills to the next level.

Create Vivid Dialogue

This manual is specifically for fiction writers who want to learn how to create riveting and compelling dialogue that propels the storyline and reveals character personality. You'll also learn how to weave emotion, description, and action into your dialogue scenes. With a special section on how to avoid the common pitfalls of writing dialogue. All of these helpful writing tools will make your dialogue sparkle!

Craft a Gripping First Chapter

This manual offers basic techniques for creating stronger beginnings and a page-turning "hook" for your fiction novel. It includes guidelines and tools for correcting common first chapter problems and it is filled with helpful examples from published novels. It provides comprehensive tips on revision and practical guidance on self-editing, which every writer needs to revise like an experienced pro.

Writing Query Letters

Writing a query letter that keeps your fiction manuscript out of the slush pile isn't easy, unless you have the tools to create a query letter that rocks! This in-depth manual includes examples of query letters with back jacket copy (blurb) for almost every fiction genre that will have an editor or agent asking for more.

Basic Plot Guide

This manual is specifically for fiction writers who want to learn how to create dramatic and comprehensible plots that have veered off course. Learn how to blend character ARC with story ARC, and heighten each scene by building suspense and how to include character goals, create tension, and increase suspense in every chapter. If you want to take your writing to the next level, then this book can help guide you in the right direction.

Back Jacket Copy

This manual contains valuable tips and tools on how to write an enticing book blurb (back jacket copy) that both self-published authors can use to lure readers into finding out more about their books, and it will help unpublished writers querying agents to hook their reader. A book description (found on the back of a novel or as a marketing tool online) is one of the most important selling tools an author can have for their self-published book. Or if you're a writer sending out query letters to literary agents, then you definitely need a strong enough "hook" to get their attention, and this guide should hopefully inspire you.

How to Get Book Reviews the WRITE Way

This comprehensive guide to marketing a book is perfect for self-published writers publishing their first novel or experienced authors trying to gain a wider readership. It includes valuable tips on networking and how to get more book reviews. And the manual explains how successful authors use social media to connect with potential readers, book reviewers, and how to sell more books. It also contains wonderful advice on how to best promote your work from established authors and recommendations by popular book bloggers on how to get your work reviewed. Whether you're a multi-published author looking to expand your audience, or a brand new author, this book will give you the tools to market your book(s) like a pro!

ON SALE NOW AT ALL MAJOR ONLINE RETAILERS

LOST IN STARLIGHT

YA Romance by Sherry Soule!

***

High school is tough. Romance with a sexy alien—even tougher.

Star reporter Sloane Masterson knows she has one helluva story when she witnesses hottie Hayden Lancaster bending forks with his mind.

Like any good journalist, Sloane sets out to uncover the truth, even if it includes a little stalking. When the superhuman feats start to pile up and the undeniable heat rises between them, Hayden has no choice but to reveal his secret: he's an alien hybrid.

They're as different as night and day—she's a curvy, purple-haired, horror junkie and he's a smoking hot, antisocial, brainiac—yet the intense fascination between them refuses to go away. Even at Hayden's insistence that dating each other is "off limits" and crazy dangerous, their fiery attraction threatens to go supernova.

Now Sloane's dealing with creepy government agents, über snobby extraterrestrials, and getting a crash course on the rules of interstellar dating. But Sloane must decide if their star -crossed romance is worth risking her own life....

BEAUTIFULLY BROKEN

YA Paranormal Romance by Sherry Soule!

"…a fun, intense, super sexy read, that lovers of Paranormal Romance will devour! Trent was my kind of bad-boy. And, can you say sexy? Shiloh and Trent's relationship was steamy to the max. Major swoon. It definitely makes me want to read the next installment." -YA Bound

The breathtaking first installment of the popular Spellbound saga is the start of Shiloh's harrowing journey into a terrifying world of magic and haunting romance…

A new guy in town. Rumors of witchcraft. And doomed first love. This is where the saga begins. . . .

Fallen Oaks isn't like other small towns, it's a secret community nestled deep within the woods, where forces of both good and evil reside.

And Shiloh Trudell isn't like other sixteen-year-old girls. She's a heritage witch with psychic powers, who can communicate with the dead. So when she takes a summer job at the haunted Craven Manor, her life takes a frightening turn after she encounters a ghost with a serious attitude problem, and an even more sinister agenda.

As if things weren't complicated enough, enter smokin' hot Trent Donovan, a boy who makes her heart pump faster and yearn for some normalcy. But after stumbling upon a supernatural murder mystery that only she can solve, she sees her chance for an ordinary life slipping even further away.

Between dating the hottest guy in town, fending off soul-sucking demons, and studying magick, Shiloh finds herself on the verge of uncovering a shocking secret that the other witches in town have vowed to protect at all costs.

But will exposing this evil coven come at a deadly price?

Buy your copy today to find out!

IMMORTAL ECLIPSE

Adult Paranormal Romance by Sherry Soule!

***

Inheriting a haunted California estate is one thing. Getting hot and bothered by its sexy caretaker is another. But Skylar Blackwell draws the line at voodoo and murder...

Twenty-four year old, Skylar would rather dive into the latest fashion magazine than a murder mystery. But when her last remaining relative is crudely sliced up with a mosaic of eerie symbols on his chest, Skylar's on a mission to find answers.

Not only are the inhabitants less than welcoming, but Summerwind's gorgeous caretaker, Dorian Delacroix—a man broken and tormented by his past—instantly ignites fiery sensations within her. And romance was definitely not on the agenda.

As she begins questioning the staff, they start dying under mysterious circumstances, and although Skylar's determined to unravel the dark history of the mansion, nothing about this place —or this enigmatic man—is what it seems.

From the moment Skylar steps foot inside Summerwind, she's plunged into a strange world of doppelgangers, voodoo rituals, haunting nightmares, and a body count that's piling up faster than her collection of Jimmy Choos. Despite her simmering desire for Dorian and their rising passion for each other, Skylar realizes that she can't really trust anyone. The only thing she knows for certain is that she needs to gather enough courage to fight the darker forces she never believed existed.

ABOUT THE AUTHOR

Sherry Soule has been a freelance developmental editor for over eight years. She has edited several award winning and NY Times bestselling novels. Sherry specializes in editing both adult and young adult genres. She hopes her insight into the creative writing process will help other writers to find success.

Please feel free to browse Sherry's blog, which has some great tips on creative writing, or if you want to contact Sherry for more info on her professional editing services, please visit her online: www. fictionwritingtools.blogspot.com

Made in the USA
San Bernardino, CA
02 November 2015